WIDEN
THE LENS

HIDDEN FORCES THAT SHAPE KIDS

by **KERRY GALARZA,** MS OTR/L

ENDORSEMENTS

"Reading this as both a therapist and mom, I gained so much insight and felt like I had finally been handed the perfect resource. The amount of candidness and realness in this work is impressive. I can't wait to pass this around to colleagues and friends alike."

- **DARCY JOSEPHSON**, Speech-Language Pathologist & Early Childhood Interventionist

"The delicacy with which Kerry is able to encourage parents and caregivers to reflect on the environmental impact - positive and negative - on their children, all while making sure that readers don't feel judged or criticized, is remarkable. I feel that this book deserves two full read-throughs - one to absorb all that it is, and a second to decide which area(s) resonate most with the family's needs so that adjustments can be made. Then, the book can be used as a continual resource throughout the parenting journey."

- **RACHEL MORRIS**, Educational Intervention & Learning Behavioral Specialist

"Very helpful in gaining insight into my son's behavior and motivations. It gave me a new perspective on how he navigates through each day. I have a much better understanding of what I can control, and how I can better support him as he grows and changes."

- **MARY LOU EISENHAUER**, Parent

"A great read - I often had to remind myself to take notes since I was moving too quickly! It's clear Kerry knows what she's talking about both as a parent and professional."

- **RACHEL SUPRENANT**, Licensed Clinical Social Worker

"It comes across on each and every page that Kerry cares deeply about consciously supporting her children and all of the children she comes in contact with as a practitioner."

- MARKUS KIRSCHNER, Educator and Writer

"As the parent of three kids and a social worker who has treated countless families over the past four decades, everything that I believe about raising healthy kids is in this book. This is simply the best book out there on parenting. Read it and let it change your life. Share it and let it change the lives of the people you care about."

- **STEVE RITTER**, Founder/Executive Director of The Midwest Institute and Center for Workplace Innovation

"Invaluable for better understanding my children and my family. It was wonderful to walk away with actionable next steps to further help my children in their growth and development."

- **CARA MILIANTI**, Licensed Clinical Social Worker

"The real examples Kerry gave from her own parenting experience are very relatable. I don't care how many times you hear it, it never gets old to hear that parenting experts struggle with what to do with their own kids too. It's ALWAYS nice to feel the reassurance that parenting is hard for all of us, even the ones who are supposed to have all the answers! I plan to use Kerry's 10 bullet points at the end to reference when I find myself getting wrapped up in my own anxieties about my children's behaviors or developmental struggle."

- **KERRY FALLON**, Occupational Therapist

For bulk orders, please call 630.832.6155 or
email booksales@teamclock.com

Published by Center for Team Excellence.

ISBN: 978-0-9890132-7-7
www.CenterforTeamExellence.com

Printed In The United States of America.

Table of Contents

INTRODUCTION

Prepare yourself: I'm about to propose something controversial. And I'm going to admit something surprising in the process. Ready? Child development professionals—including myself—tend to go about things all wrong. Well, maybe not *all* wrong. But many of us have fallen into the habit of overlooking something critically important.

> *The precious child at the focus of our well-intentioned, evaluative gaze embodies so much more than what we see in front of us. We frequently forget that they are always woven into a complicated tapestry of social, structural, physiological, and emotional influences. While mostly invisible, those influences shape the child every moment of every day.*

During my career as a pediatric occupational therapist, I've noticed time and again that the emphasis on child development tends to rest heavily on skill acquisition and performance. Whenever there are speed bumps to growth, plans are made to remedy the problem through direct teaching of skills.

The teaching can be successful, but it's missing that huge piece of the puzzle: the countless influences of the environment. A child's environment *always* has a significant impact on their foundations for learning, capacity for connection, potential for lasting growth, and a resilience that can support adaptation. The benefits of our support methods are so much richer whenever we're able to grasp the whole picture. We are doing our kids a huge disservice by not addressing all of the vital aspects of growth, behavior, and learning.

My colleague Steve Ritter and I developed the Family Environmental Assessment Tool (F.E.A.T.) in 2020 to address the gap. Published under the title *Elevating Your Kid's Growth: The Family Environmental Assessment Tool*, the assessment booklet offers a simple way of measuring subtle influences in kids' development so that parents and professionals alike can identify early chances to address problem spots and capture growth opportunities.

Using the model helps shine a light on areas that could use attention, and perhaps more importantly, it raises some new questions about the impact of the environment and family on learning. It's designed to provide a jumping-off point to help you choose the right actions for the right moments for your child. But here's the thing: assessing the impact of your kid's environment is only the first step. So then what?

This book will help you determine where to start, provide methods for deciding what to change, and help you know when it's time to bring in extra resources.

After a brief overview in Chapter 1, Chapters 2–9 will walk you through each of the eight aspects of a child's world that contribute to their behavior and development: *health, family expectations, family dynamics, caregiver needs, developmental stage, enablers & obstacles, support systems, and disposition.* These chapters are further broken down into sections with tips for identifying impacts, widening the lens, taking action, and making it stick. Chapter 10 will bring it all together.

Some of the chapters will be useful right away, and others won't. Feel free to skim or skip around. Make notes in the margins and dog-ear things that resonate or give you pause. Allow this book to be a dynamic, universal tool that you can leverage throughout your child's life as they continue to grow and change. It might not be the best book to share once you've marked it up and bent pages, but that's the idea. Allow it to etch a groove into your reference shelf.

CHAPTER 1

THE IMPACT OF ENVIRONMENT

When was the last time you stopped—I mean really stopped dead in your tracks—to take in your child? To absorb all of the wonderful peculiarities that make them so uniquely who they are? Maybe it was when you peeked in on them sleeping angelically before you turned in for the night. Perhaps it was during a rare moment of quiet as they played near you. Maybe it's hard to even remember. I'm willing to bet it wasn't when chaos was unfolding all around you or when your child's behavior made your teeth clench. How about the details of the scene surrounding them—did you take time to observe all of the little things contributing to their behavior?

Life moves at a dizzying pace while we're embroiled in the many tasks of raising and caring for young kids. Add the myriad complications—family drama, illness, any of life's curveballs—to the mix, and it can feel nearly impossible to keep up.

We all miss many things that become important in hindsight. This can be especially true when it comes to compatibility between our kids and the influences they face. Having a set of guidelines to break things down into parts helps us pay better attention to the people, things, and interactions that deserve our attention—all within the moments that matter most.

THE FAMILY ENVIRONMENTAL ASSESSMENT TOOL—A QUICK OVERVIEW

Note: While it's not a requirement to use the following tool to understand how the environment is acting on your child, sometimes it helps to have a visual aid to organize your thoughts. Even if a particular section doesn't apply today, chances are you'll be referencing it later, as all of these environmental domains tend to ebb and flow in most families.

Using an environmental lens is based on the understanding that growth occurs in cycles:

- A strong **foundation** enables kids to connect effectively.
- These **connections** provide avenues of growth.
- **Growth**, in turn, makes the kid more resilient.
- **Resilience**, of course, further strengthens the foundation.

And around they go again!

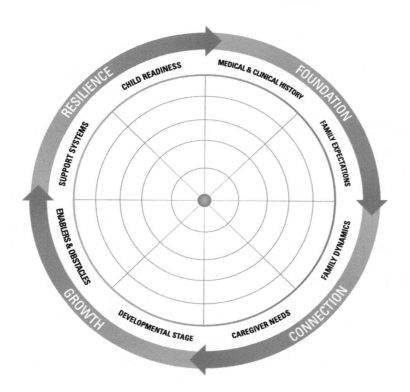

This environment assessment circle is designed to provide a simple, straightforward way to discover how each environmental factor is impacting growth at any point in time.

At each stage of the foundation-connection-growth-resilience cycle, there are important environmental factors that are best managed when they're understood and measured. As the cycle progresses, advances in each stage are delivered to the next stage. Likewise, the consequences of missed opportunities are also carried forward.

Here's a quick rundown of each phase of the circle.

FOUNDATION

In the FOUNDATION stage, we're looking at health and family expectations.

HEALTH: Health has a powerful influence when it comes to engagement. Sometimes a health problem is acting as an actual barrier to connection and growth, as when illness or pain prevents a child or a caregiver from interaction. But even when that's not the case, health troubles can still interfere in subtle but key ways (distractibility, irritability). This is also where we take any established medical conditions or clinical concerns, past or present, into account.

FAMILY EXPECTATIONS: To maintain a strong foundation, it's important to understand how each family member's expectations for your child align. This can also include other people in your child's inner circle. What exactly do each of you consider to be priorities for your child? Is there anything that needs "fixing," and what are each of your ideas about how to make this happen? What would each of you want to tackle first if there were competing priorities? Which players would you each like to see take an active role and why?

As you ask these questions, make sure you're keeping them on a small scale. Try your best to narrow your focus to one set of circumstances at a time (e.g., bedtime tantrums). Even though some themes are probably common throughout your family's daily experiences, it's wise to pick just one specific challenge at a time to get the most complete understanding of exactly what's going on.

Some other common examples:

- Your child is falling apart after 2 minutes of homework.
- Your preschooler can't sit still for dinner.
- You're desperate to find ways for your kids to play nicely to-

gether so you can get something (anything!) done.

  ✦   Your adolescent is struggling to manage their responsibilities independently.

Each of these might seem like mere roadblocks around a bigger issue ("My kid won't listen!") but the most enduring progress is always made by fully tackling one problem before moving on to the next.

CONNECTION

A strong and unified foundation paves the way for kids to be able to connect. The CONNECTION stage highlights the impact of family dynamics and caregiver needs.

FAMILY DYNAMICS: Connection looks different for every family and each relationship. What matters most is family members are understanding each other's needs when it comes to engagement. Healthy connection also means everyone is doing their best to respect and make time and space for one another.

CAREGIVER NEEDS: An adult's physical and emotional needs are equally as vital as their child's. When a parent or a caregiver's needs go unmet, they're unable to fully "show up" for the child.

GROWTH

A stable foundation and strong interpersonal connections lead to more opportunities for a child to experience GROWTH, where we focus on the influence of developmental stage and enablers & obstacles.

DEVELOPMENTAL STAGE: A child's developmental stage includes all of their cognitive, physical, social-emotional, and adaptive skills. These skills influence the way they're able to respond to support and react to their surroundings.

ENABLERS & OBSTACLES: The fit between a child's developmental stage and the quality of environmental enablers or obstacles dictates the scope of their growth potential. Enablers and obstacles vary per household, family, and moment in time, but include things like safety, technology, social media, sensory stimulation, routines, and schedules.

RESILIENCE

Growth enables RESILIENCE, which is fed through personal support systems and child readiness (disposition or personality). Strong resilience reinforces the foundation for the next phase.

SUPPORT SYSTEMS: Support systems refer to your family's access to community resources, professional networks, friendships, and neighborhood relationships. Having adequate support promotes your family's ability to be flexible and adapt to needs, both emotional and logistical. A healthy support system will evolve as kids grow and families' needs change.

CHILD READINESS: Child readiness refers to your child's ability to participate in and adapt to their experiences. It's a sum of their traits, such as curiosity, perseverance, initiative, self-discipline, adventurousness, self-awareness, confidence, playfulness, the ability to reflect, and desire for engagement. We often refer to this unique mix as their disposition or personality. Readiness also includes your child's capacity for trust, an awareness of their emerging knowledge base and their attitudes toward learning.

It's important to note that the goal isn't to change your child's wiring but to ensure that any routines, plans, or changes you make are tailored to promote their desire for participation.

USING THE ENVIRONMENTAL ASSESSMENT CIRCLE

WHO: This simple environmental assessment can be used by parents or self-administered by adolescents. It is suitable for families with children of all ages and abilities.

WHAT: The purpose is to visualize how well each phase is being fulfilled by your circumstances. A wedge is only partially filled if it represents an area for growth. The more full it is, the more it is an area of strength. After you've gone around the circle, you'll have a clear visual of your family's priority areas for attention.

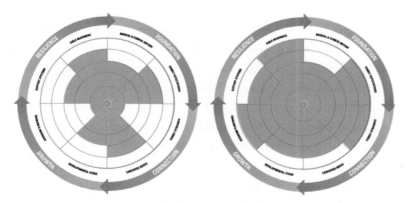

Please refer to the F.E.A.T. booklet for detailed instructions about how to use this tool.

WHERE: The model can be easily applied anywhere. Depending on the age of your child and your circumstances, this might be at home, at school, or in a daycare setting.

WHEN: Aspects of the environment may be stable for a while, followed by rapid changes. When we fail to pay attention to small changes, we limit our kids' potential for growth. Regular tracking of subtle changes leads to more effective learning opportunities. With this in mind, there is no prescribed timeline. You can pull out the assessment whenever you feel like you need a little more clarity on the elements that are impacting your child's day.

SEEKING HELP

Once you've figured out areas that could use some attention, do you address things by yourself or partner with professionals? Positive change is prompted either by activating existing family resources, engaging a partnership with a professional, or some combination of the two.

Many of the environmental influences highlighted by the assessment exercise will involve things that can be addressed on your own. If, for example, your child's academic performance has suffered lately and the assessment reveals that there's been escalated conflict between parents since a recent trauma, addressing the conflict will eventually have a positive impact on your child's school engagement.

Sometimes issues uncovered by your assessment will require outside resources. "It takes a village to raise a child" isn't just an abstract proverb—it speaks a truth, regardless of your particular circumstances. Engaging professional consultation when the path isn't clear can open avenues to problem-solving.

Your solution may be to tap into the expertise of someone who is currently waiting in the wings. Perhaps that's a friend who has had a similar experience, a grandparent, an uncle, or a therapist you've already brought into your circle. Our best resources are often right under our noses.

Either way, small changes can make big differences.

IDENTIFYING CHALLENGES

Once you have a better idea about which environmental aspects (internal and external) of your child's world could use a boost, you're primed to take it a step further. Think about what might be contributing to the problem spots. Put names to the things that aren't working and the things that should be addressed.

Find time to have conversations with your family about what you see, even when the talks might be uncomfortable. When your lens widens to the entire family, surprising contributions to the challenges raised on the assessment may crop up. It's a common understanding in family therapy circles that every family member's behavior serves an important function for the family as a whole. A child's "acting up," for example, may be serving the purpose of distracting from marital conflict. Which is the problem and which is the symptom?

Changing old patterns can be hard. It's helpful to begin by acknowledging any initial resistance and then agreeing to try to push through it together. Families are ecosystems and, by nature, seek sameness (homeostasis) even if staying the same isn't healthy.

Blinders can be especially difficult to remove if they've been serving a protective function. If you enter the conversation knowing that the end goal is to support all of the players in the process, it will be much more productive. Work together to see how things could be better for both your child and your whole family; then use that vision as encouragement and fuel whenever you're feeling stuck or discouraged.

DESIGNING ACTIONS

If you have more than one trouble spot, decide which makes sense to address first. Oftentimes, there will be a conspicuous need. An epiphany is only an epiphany until it's revealed—at which time it becomes obvious. If an obvious area requires attention, go ahead and pull it to the forefront for planning.

You can get the ball rolling by either making small tweaks or crafting bigger changes. The right course really depends on your unique circumstances. A vital piece to this initial decision lies in two areas: Family Expectations and Child Readiness.

If either of these areas are sticking points toward progress, you may want to raise them to the top of the pile for attention. Until key teammates are ready to participate, any other priorities are going to be stalled in some way. You can't win if you don't play, and the win's harder to get when you're short teammates.

A "low-hanging fruit" approach is useful. If you notice an area for improvement even in the "pretty much OK" areas, by all means, go for it. An example: The Caregiver Needs area is looking good and it isn't a big concern, but thinking about it triggered the idea to begin waking up a few minutes earlier to start your day from a calmer place before the morning chaos begins. This little bit of parent self-care doesn't require much planning or coordination, and it's bound to have a positive impact on your child's morning as well.

Following along with the low-hanging fruit approach, the Enablers & Obstacles area usually has some easy tune-ups as well. I haven't met a family yet—including mine—who couldn't constantly benefit from some small tweaks. Things as simple as removing video game access on weekdays (worked for my family!) or putting some crayons and paper where your child likes to hang out so they can color (and build skills) can make a big difference in the flow of your day.

Bliss By Harry Bliss

"What are you doing?! Where are your crayons?!"

SUMMARY

The environmental assessment circle is unique in its ability to capture the cyclical nature of developmental change, rather than charting it as purely linear. Each cycle forms a new foundation of strengths, enables the ability to connect, feeds growth, and empowers resilience. When one pillar is well-established and secure, the next phase of the cycle is optimized.

The opposite is also true: when gaps occur along the way, the missing pieces will impact the following phases. The goal of the model is to help you identify some of the more subtle opportunities for repair so that each part of the cycle can be strengthened by the others.

CHAPTER 2

YOUR CHILD'S & FAMILY'S HEALTH

IDENTIFYING THE IMPACT

As you think about your family's health, you might need to rewind a little. The goal here is to establish an understanding of how health is contributing to your child's and family's functioning, including any relevant health problems your family experienced in the past. There may be no health concerns that are impacting your family at all. If that's the case, wonderful! But if your child has a diagnosis or has been dancing around one, or if there have been health concerns of any other nature within the family, you might want to pay special attention to this section.

Begin by asking yourself a couple of questions to lay the groundwork for understanding how health needs are influencing your child:

- ✦ How much experience has your child had with the medical/

clinical community up to this point?

- How have health concerns impacted your child's development (if at all)?

Then zoom out for a wider picture:

- What kind of experience has the rest of the family had with
the medical/clinical community?
- Has this contributed to your understanding of any current
difficulties you're having with your child?
- Have past health concerns colored family members' feelings
about what's going on today?

If established health factors are contributing to your child's ability to learn, connect, or grow, they are foundational when addressing
other elements of the developmental cycle. Carefully weigh any current interventions and their value. Do you have the right people on
your healthcare team? Consider how the interventions are progressing.
Keeping a rhythm with familiar treatments and strategies can be com-
forting. However, there may be some benefit from making changes, if
not entirely redrawing the blueprint.

Take a good look at all of your family's medical/clinical interactions. How have they impacted your feelings about any current situations? You may want to begin by thinking about your interactions
with your pediatrician. Parents are usually given information about
expected growth at check-ups, but there may or may not be any meaningful conversation around it. Have you felt supported and that your
child has really been "seen" by their doctor? Ask yourself if you've felt
listened to. Then apply the same question to any other specialists in
your circle.

Worries about development are often quelled by knowing that at least one trusted person understands what's going on with your child. There's tremendous benefit in finding someone who can genuinely partner with you on ways to address any health or developmental concerns you may have. On the other hand, if you've received limited, impersonal feedback or felt misunderstood by the medical community, frustrations become amplified and can leave you feeling lost, suspicious, or both. Take heart in the likelihood that a better fit is out there, and it may not be as hard to find as you think.

MEDICAL, CLINICAL, OR A BLEND OF BOTH?

*A **medical condition** refers to a disease, illness, injury, genetic or congenital defect, or biological or psychological condition that lies outside the range of typical age-appropriate variation. Examples are physical disabilities, developmental disorders, intellectual disabilities, language and learning disorders, attention disorders, vision impairment, and hearing loss.*

*A **clinical concern** refers to a pattern of performance characterized by observable behaviors or symptoms that interfere with functioning. Examples are sensory processing differences, anxiety and depressive behaviors that interfere with day-to-day routines, oppositional/conduct difficulties, attentional difficulties, and emotional regulation difficulties.*

You may find that a medical condition is either creating or contributing to a related clinical concern. It's also possible for clinical concerns to become diagnosed medical conditions over time. In any case, it's important to have the right people in place to support your family in developing and maintaining an appropriate intervention plan when necessary for your child.

WHAT IF I'M NOT SURE?

Many parents of younger children lose sleep wondering if there's a medical or clinical problem that hasn't yet been identified. We live in the information era, but there are pitfalls to having unlimited access to web-based material.

> *It's frighteningly easy to get sucked in by the infinite online symptom-checkers, milestones charts, and parent forums. Be careful not to compulsively click things that stoke anxieties and offer contradicting advice.*

I'm a confessed research addict. When I became pregnant for the first time, I dove headfirst into every pool of knowledge available to me on prenatal development. During one memorable conversation, my mother-in-law warned me that I might be "harming my baby by worrying too much."

My information consumption ramped up after my son arrived and, if I'm honest, I became a bit obsessive. This went on until I realized I was completely exhausting myself. Around the same time, I figured out I wasn't doing my son any favors by distracting myself with hypothetical concerns—when he was right in front of me showing me everything I needed to know.

> *Nobody knows your child better than you do. If your gut is telling you that your child's struggles might be better addressed with medical intervention or clinical therapy in the mix, be confident in that thought.*

If you need to spend some (limited!) time scouring the internet for bits of evidence to feel empowered with information, go for it. But then make sure to take the critical step of making the phone calls or writing emails to medical and clinical experts who can assess your child and provide you with personal, directed, and trusted feedback. Be the driver—not the passenger—in this car.

In my experience, the hardest part is getting the ball rolling. Once you've decided it's time to seek an outside helper, your next move is to locate a good fit. This can be accomplished by using online resources, asking trusted contacts for leads, and doing some simple outreach.

It may feel like a daunting job at the outset, but more often than not, you'll be surprised to find the help you need is sitting close by— maybe just a phone call or email away. And remember: "expert" opinion should always be filtered by your instinct as a parent or caregiver. This gets you off on the right foot.

WIDENING THE LENS

The current impact of a health concern will steer your plans. And by current, I mean *this moment*. Children change at a wild pace, even when we aren't checking off obvious milestones on a skills chart. Your kid today isn't the kid you had yesterday. Therefore, a health concern's impact can change just as rapidly.

Depending on the nature of your child's health concern, their internal/body environment will be regularly shifting alongside baseline neurological function, individual chemistry, and naturally occurring physical maturation. In some cases, a medical or clinical concern might even have onset during one developmental stage, but symptoms might not rise to the surface until a later stage (when the emergence of a new ability becomes a requirement).

Recognition of these near-constant changes may feel overwhelming at first, but your job here is simple. Consider your child from a health concern perspective, and mentally scan only for factors that can be realistically influenced right now. How can you best intervene to lessen obstacles and grow opportunities? Adding more intervention isn't always the answer. In fact, maybe the opposite is true. Sometimes there's wisdom in clearing the plate a little, even temporarily.

> *We all know how it feels to be overwhelmed with too many demands and expectations in our day. Our children aren't immune to that weight.*

Those who are asked to participate in regular interventions as a result of a medical condition or clinical concern—sometimes since birth—tend to have less breathing room built in to their days than their peers. Unstructured free time to play and work through the skills we've been teaching our children is essential to healthy development. Depending on the nature of interventions, the seeds that were planted during therapy or treatment may require a little time and space for successful germination to occur.

On the other hand, you may be thinking that the amount of intervention you have in place feels appropriate and sustainable, but some strategies or services are missing the mark. Adding to or altering your professional team could be the answer. Ideally, a child's medical and clinical support system will flex in response to ebbing and flowing priorities. Temporarily giving the stage to one medical/clinical intervention over another may have a positive impact. This might mean elevating one of the interventions you already have in place or adding a new intervention altogether for a time.

> *Don't be afraid to try something new—nothing needs to be set in stone.*

A third possibility is that doing a mental assessment of today's circumstances will spark an "ah-ha." Now could be the right moment to seek out medical or clinical support for the first time. If this is the case, begin by tapping the resources most readily available. Talk to trusted friends, family members, and professionals in your child's life (e.g., teachers, care providers).

Are they seeing the same things? Who do they have in their network who might be able to help? Put some feelers out, and trust your instincts. You don't need to have a fully developed plan on day one. Start small and see where it takes you. You can always make changes.

TAKING ACTION

Let's put your insights and observations to use. Medical conditions and clinical concerns impact your child's capacity for growth situation-by-situation. Pick an event or time of day you'd like to improve. The degree of impact will depend on the mixture of these elements:

- How the concern affects your child's engagement and learning.
- The intervention your child is currently receiving.
- Aspects of the situation you hope to address (e.g., participation in a community park district class).

Try to break down each of these elements. Write it out, even. Maybe there's not much of a medical/clinical impact on your circumstances after all. Or you might find that medical or clinical factors appear to be driving most of whatever difficulty you're currently encountering.

Shift your focus to determine whether the degree of impact is something you can influence. You may already have an appropriate intervention plan in place to address your child's medical and clinical needs. If so, use your newfound clarity to reignite a conversation with your medical and clinical partners.

If there's an opportunity to update goals and upgrade interventions to better suit your child's position on the environment-growth cycle, seize it. And if you don't have a medical/clinical intervention or plan in place yet and think your child could benefit from one, do the prep work to make it happen. There's no time like the present.

CASE EXAMPLE:

Cora's parents hit the ground running the moment she was born. She came into the world early with low birth weight. They barely had a chance to look at her before she was swept away to the neonatal intensive care unit (NICU).

Cora spent the next couple months of her life in the hospital hooked up to equipment. Her parents had to negotiate all of Cora's medical interventions while trying to get to know their daughter. And all within limited time frames and under the watchful eye of NICU staff.

Cora's parents were young and inexperienced when she was born. Because of their age, they often felt that medical personnel took a dismissive, "expert" tone with them. Over time, they came to expect interactions with the medical community to feel condescending. They also came to understand that their abilities as parents were often underestimated.

As Cora grew into toddlerhood, she continued to receive medical and clinical services to help support her growth. The services were based in multiple different systems: a pediatrician from one healthcare system, a dietician from another, developmental therapies through the state early intervention program, and home health nursing from an outside private agency.

The result was that Cora's parents were getting all sorts of advice and recommendations that didn't always match. They were also tasked with managing multiple clinicians and interventions. It felt like a full-time job. It was taking a toll on everyone, including 3-year old Cora, who regularly engaged in power struggles with her parents and professionals alike.

After a couple years of this, Cora's mom began to realize that her impulse to take on so much responsibility came from two places: her desire to give Cora every possible opportunity and her wish to prove herself competent. Once she began to take a closer look at the actual value of each intervention from the first desire only—"Does this provide the best opportunity to maximize my daughter's potential *right now?*"—she began to winnow down the list.

Her decision to pull back was reinforced by Cora's positive response. Her protest behaviors gradually reduced, and her interaction during family time became much richer. The extra downtime and reduced stress load ended up having a restorative impact on each member of the family.

MAKING IT STICK

Once a decision has been made to initiate a change in medical or clinical intervention, it's time to execute. Depending on what your family has decided, this might be a small step, such as reaching out to a new clinician to ask questions and receive feedback. Or it might mean shifting your focus and priorities to better reflect today's circumstances and your child's needs. Whatever your steps, the most important (and often hardest) thing is to get started. After you make that first phone call or send that first email, momentum tends to take over.

Plan to regularly reassess the fit of any medical and clinical intervention you've decided to put in place. Needs will change as time goes on. The aim is to maintain flexibility. This can be difficult when the health landscape is changing quickly.

Proactive change isn't a concept that is usually tied to the way we think about medical and clinical intervention. We all tend to stick to a medical plan once it's in place, in part due to comfort with routine and in part to let it "take effect." But given the constant shifts kids experience as they grow, it's essential for their intervention plans to be able to shift regularly right along with them.

HOW WILL I KNOW ISSUES HAVE BEEN SUCCESSFULLY ADDRESSED?

Although each child's circumstances are very different, there are a couple of failsafe signs that you've made a move in the right direction. Consider the answer to two questions:

- Have any symptoms or behaviors lessened or improved in response to treatment changes (or the addition of treatment for the first time)?
- Have any changes positively impacted stress levels and the way your child/family moves through the day?

Even when consulting a group of experts, no one knows your child better than you. You know whether things are easing or worsening. You know whether the chemistry feels right with your circle of professionals. See yourself as the expert even during periods of self-doubt. Trust your instincts.

CHAPTER 3

YOUR FAMILY'S EXPECTATIONS

IDENTIFYING THE IMPACT

Now we're going to take a look at two closely intertwined parts: each family member's expectations for your child, plus any bigger-picture family goals. Spoiler alert: they don't always reflect the same priorities.

As we're all aware, the make-up of each family is unique. Whether you choose to consider grandparents, aunts, uncles, or cousins while thinking about the topics we'll explore here depends on their level of involvement in your child's life. Babysitters, nannies, daycare providers, and other regular caregivers can also play a big part in the day-to-day life of your family. If this is true for you, don't hesitate to include them.

One by one, find out each person's main priorities for your child. What kinds of growth do they wish to see? Are there any behaviors they want to fix? These are vital questions. Another vital question: Do they even think change is possible?

Have actual conversations about what everyone envisions for your child. Allow each person to describe what an ideal alternative to current behaviors would look like. Encourage them to be as specific as possible. There's a surprising amount of value in simply letting people put words to their viewpoints.

Kids have a knack for showing different sides of themselves to different people.

Have you ever gotten feedback from a teacher that didn't match what you've been seeing at home? Are we talking about the same child?! Or have you had a grandparent say your kid's behavior changed when you came home?

That last one is a favorite of mine, by the way. It happens to me without fail. Even today, my husband exclaimed as I walked in from the grocery store to a house shaking on its foundation from my wrestling and arguing boys, "I swear they were fine until you got here!" We've all been there.

Sometimes it seems like they save their worst behavior for home. This happens because kids have a savvy ability to read and respond to the unique players and expectations within their family and community. Of course, they save their best for their classroom teacher. And, of course, they save their worst for the place where love is unconditional.

Look at your inner circle and find out what each person sees and what they expect. After you have gathered input from your family and other key players, look for themes. This will help explain any discrepancies. Our kids adapt to their environmental expectations.

Do everyone's expectations for your child match, for the most part? If there are any outliers, don't discount them. Significant differences in expectations for your child simply warrant some more conversation. Try to find out what's behind the disparity.

See if you can get on the same page with your core desires. Even when individual priorities don't align perfectly, you'll probably be able to agree on a broader target for your child's growth, behavior, or development. Once that target is identified, figure out a way to apply it to the circumstances you are hoping to work on.

For example, your toddler might fall apart each evening at bedtime. Any veteran parent will tell you that few things can fray nerves and cause arguments as quickly as listening to prolonged screaming from your child's bedroom after tuck-in. Do you let them try to "work it out" on their own and find a way to tolerate the crying and yelling? Do you go in repeatedly and try to soothe, or just let them sleep with you? If siblings are being subjected to the noise, this will further complicate things.

My youngest, the one with the biggest set of lungs, didn't consistently sleep through the night until he was 2. Somewhere in that 24-month horrible stretch of sleep deprivation, my husband and I decided (after a fair amount of debate) to let him cry it out. This lasted maybe a week until my preschooler—who shared the bedroom—complained that he was extra tired. "I'm really tired too, sweets," I replied, attempting to empathize. His eye-opening response: "But mommy, *you're* the mommy! *I'm* just a kid!" We stopped the sleep training that night.

There are dozens of books written on the topic of sleep training, and every well-meaning friend, extended family member, and child development professional will likely have conflicting recommendations on how to handle it. Odds are good that you and your partner will also have differing ideas on what to do.

You may never fully agree, but it helps to find a shred of common ground before debating the details. In this case, the target is to eventually get everyone the best night's rest possible and to establish a less nerve-shattering routine in the end. Acknowledge that you're working together on the same broad end goal, and then work backward from there.

Another factor to consider is your family's expectation about how any changes will be executed and how they will fit into your routines. We will explore that more in the next chapter, but there's some cross-over here. Decide who will be responsible for what, and how much support is expected from each family member. This will be easier now than after the train has left the station, so to speak.

ARE EXPECTATIONS REALISTIC?

This is a tough question to answer because it requires you to predict the future. Your prediction rests on two mostly unpredictable phenomena: your child's growth trajectory and human behavior. Both are moving targets.

But there are many clues available to you. Personal history, established developmental frameworks (including those specific to any medical conditions), and input from trusted individuals will help you form a realistic gauge. The patterns and themes they reveal are usually reliable predictors of your child's growth and development.

Your answers may feel mostly hypothetical, but your conclusions will be based on current evidence. You are the top expert on your child and their potential, and you have information from other experts available to you. You also already know how your family operates when working together on common goals, including which strategies tend to work best.

Try to speak the language of each player when considering a change. The goal is to get everyone on the same page.

Even though you are the expert on your child, it's normal to feel a lack of confidence when you're managing something you've never seen before. A version of "imposter syndrome" can make you hesitant to trust your instinct. We all have a small case of imposter syndrome when we are navigating uncharted waters. The only cure is to dive in so the waters get charted and our ability (and confidence) as a parent grows.

WIDENING THE LENS

Once family expectations have become clearer, turn your attention to how they're impacting your child. What you find may not always look pretty or feel satisfying. Reconciling a child's constant changes with our expectations can be a herculean task.

You'd be hard-pressed to find a parent (or therapist, or educator) on the planet who hasn't been off base at some point by either underestimating or overestimating a child's potential. Whether off base or accurate, adults project their expectations during every interaction. For better or worse, that exchange has a lot of power.

The power comes mostly from your child's read on your expectations, whether they're stated aloud or implicit. Even very young children will start to internalize messages about their abilities. As they grow, they begin to form more concrete ideas about how they are measuring up. A match between expectations and ability will promote a child's sense of self-efficacy and serve to motivate them. A mismatch will lead to frustration or a sense of inadequacy.

My middle son smiled, cooed, and connected with everyone as a baby. He could also move small furniture and climb before he was able to walk. My husband and I decided early on that he would probably be an ultra-social kid destined for athletics. We embraced that narrative well into his grade school years. We communicated it in many ways: the teams we put him on, the way we talked about him to others (within his earshot), and the pep talks we gave him to be a leader and engage with larger groups of his peers.

Then one day a comment from a close friend turned my perception on its head: "You know, I actually think he's a lot like you." Me!? An introverted, non-competitive homebody? But he was right.

I looked back at the times we expressed frustration with our son for being "unmotivated" and "antisocial" and realized he'd been showing us that part of himself for years. We'd somehow gotten stuck inside our idea of him while he kept on growing and changing. He was still a physically driven kid with a deep capacity for connection, but the expectations we projected onto him for extraversion and a strong ambition for competitive athletics simply didn't jive.

Your expectations drive the way you set up the context for performance, whether subconsciously or with intention. If you feel that your child's struggles are the result of "not trying hard enough" or "being stubborn and defiant," the support you provide them will be very different than if you attribute the struggles to a personality trait, a health concern, or a developmental root cause.

On the flipside, regularly stepping in, making allowances, and doing more than necessary will eventually deprive your child of learning new skills and developing a sense of self-efficacy. If you catch every fall, they never learn to get back up.

When we taught our oldest child how to ride a bike, I was afraid to let go of the seat for fear he would fall over. I couldn't understand why his sense of balance wasn't taking hold. When I finally let go, he did, indeed, fall over. But on his way to the ground, he tried to counterbalance his fall by leaning in the opposite direction. His next attempt, although wobbly, sent him on his way. I felt like I had learned as much as he had that day.

The tone of your expectations is also communicated passively. It's reinforced in the physical setup of your space, the toys and materials you provide, the activities you give your child, the way instructions are worded, and the amount of time you wait before anticipating your desired response. Your kids read these subtle messages even though they may not be consistent with your intent.

All of this may sound discouraging or maybe even a little scary, but the truth is that there are always opportunities for adjustment and repair whenever you discover a gap or a mismatch. Kids will almost always surprise you with their adaptability and responsiveness when a stage is reset to support their success.

TAKING ACTION

First, try to identify where there are mismatches between expectations and your child's current ability. Adults often fall into the trap of getting stuck either in past performance or future visions when they consider a child's potential. The trick is to stop and look at the child in front of you today.

Then ask yourself if you're communicating the right things. Does the environment maximize opportunities for your child to express their skills? Start with the basics. The physical environment gives clues to your expectations and is often the easiest to alter when something's not working.

> Look at your toys, materials, school work station, media distractions, and accessibility to things in your space.

These factors will be revisited later in the book, but your focus, for now, should be on simply determining how well the physical environment is reflecting your expectations for your child's performance, and to recognize what it's communicating to your child. If materials are unsuitable for your child—too easy, too difficult, or don't reflect their interests—remove them (or just shuffle them to a sibling for whom they're better suited).

The same goes for tasks. Are you regularly met with tantrums, protest behavior, or disengagement during routine activities? If so, take a moment to consider if your expectations are too high or missing the mark for the time being.

Try scaling back, offering more help, or breaking the activity down into smaller steps. If you see your child respond by showing more willingness to participate (as opposed to just letting you do it for them), you know you've made a good move. Play with the level of support until you hit a sweet spot. Then slowly reduce the amount of help you provide to build upon their skills. But remember to stay flexible—everyone has their good and bad days.

On the other hand, your child could be silently begging for more of a challenge. You might want to try letting them contribute meaningfully to a problematic routine. The thrill of ownership can be powerful. Getting to be in charge of choosing groceries at the store, helping to cook dinner, or contributing to the setup of their workspace might be just what your child wants, and exactly the trick you need to gain cooperation.

When a child of any age experiences success in an activity that's appropriately challenging and stimulating, there's really nothing better. The feeling of confidence, engagement, and energy that comes from accomplishment is infinitely rewarding. And it's the best path to deeper, more lasting learning. These small achievements multiply.

There is one more important action to take once you've identified your family's expectations and refined the fit with your child: share your findings with the other caregivers and healthcare providers in your child's life (if any). And don't be shy about letting them know exactly what you expect from them. That also goes for your expectations about the kind of help you hope they'll provide. Getting everyone on the same page lays the groundwork for your child's future success.

Andre entered the world as the picture of health, and his family was overjoyed. All of their hopes and dreams had come true. However, as Andre developed, he began demonstrating subtle signs of sensory processing difficulties and language deficits. While his mother Imani acknowledged some differences, she felt they were within the scope of typical development—possibly even the indication of above-average intelligence and creativity.

At times, she became defensive. She admitted that when anyone suggested he might benefit from support services, she immediately flipped on her "mama bear switch" and set them straight. Not everyone saw this side of Imani. Andre's dad was most often on the receiving end. He worried about Andre all the time.

He frequently pointed out that Andre wasn't getting along with his same-age cousins, and he pushed them to interact more. In his experience, extended family was supposed to be close. His son was missing out on an important part of childhood. Imani chose to dismiss the cousin playdates because, as she put it, "Dre just wasn't into them."

But as Andre grew older, Imani began receiving feedback from his preschool and daycare teachers that he was falling behind and unable to participate in some social activities. After talking it over, his parents eventually decided to tap into a small network of child development professionals. If nothing else, Imani rationalized, doing so might help Andre's teachers better understand and access his unique talents.

Maybe it would help him play better with his cousins in the process, too. Their feedback slowly began to shift Imani's understanding of his behaviors. Perhaps he could benefit from some support, after all.

While she wasn't interested in putting a label on anything, she carefully began to build a plan for adding extra assistance into Andre's routines. This steady and measured approach proved very effective. Imani was deliberate in her choices.

She regularly made changes to his circle of helpers when she felt there wasn't an ideal fit or that Andre wasn't fully benefiting from their help based on his developmental needs. The result was a small, core team who she felt really "knew" her son and his potential, and also respected her expectations and priorities. Everyone in her circle had good intentions, but not all guidance was helpful.

She was careful to filter the often-overwhelming flow of advice and recommendations she received from well-meaning friends, family members, and clinicians. She prided herself on being a "tough sell" and strove to adopt changes only after thorough research and reflection with her family. Most things didn't end up making the cut.

While she knew her approach didn't necessarily resemble those of many other parents in her online developmental forums or in the clinic waiting room, it worked for her. And Andre seemed to respond well to the few select strategies she did choose to pursue. Imani learned to trust her instinct.

MAKING IT STICK

Let's say you've already done the hard work of clarifying and coordinating everyone's primary expectations, and you've also made adjustments to best reflect your goals and your child's needs and abilities. Your task at this point is to facilitate smaller, more frequent check-ins with all family members, caregivers, and anyone else within your child's inner circle. Let these questions guide you during the check-ins:

1. Are we still sharing the same (or similar) expectations for our child and for any goals we have?
2. Are our expectations still appropriate, given our child's response and growth?
3. Do we agree on any tweaks that could be made?

If any answers seem to have sticking points, just take a couple steps back and spend extra time with them. Your child's abilities and responses are always morphing, so your expectations need to morph alongside them. You're bound to be playing catch-up from time to time. Usually, a little recalibration is all that's needed to get back on track.

HOW WILL I KNOW ISSUES HAVE BEEN SUCCESSFULLY ADDRESSED?

The clues to success will be found in your family and child's comfort level. Measure how things are feeling, along with the positive growth, learning, and behaviors seen in your child. A match between expectations and reality should feel good to everyone.

If someone is demonstrating signs of frustration, dissatisfaction, or stress, it's time to go back to the drawing board. This usually doesn't mean a total scrap of plans—simply an edit or two. Regroup whenever you feel more work can be done to get team members realigned with one another and with your child's current abilities.

CHAPTER 4

YOUR FAMILY'S DYNAMICS

IDENTIFYING THE IMPACT

Just as every family has a unique member make-up, all family members also have unique ways of interacting with one another. Anyone who has experienced a blending of families through romance or marriage knows the obvious truth of this. But the far-reaching impact of family dynamics on our kids can be less obvious.

Personalities, parenting philosophies, world views, and communication styles are bound to vary with each member of your household and extended family—oftentimes significantly. These differences are expected and inevitable. In fact, it's this very mix of unique characteristics that strengthens family bonds when things are working well. It also accounts for some of the barriers and tensions that can form around a variety of issues.

Picture your family like a web. Each satellite person is connected to each of the others by lines. The lines represent different interaction styles. The lines drawn between the members can be thin, thick, wavy, dotted, or broken—the way you represent the interactions is up to you, but as you imagine them, look for patterns. Some people will be consistent with the way they interact. Some will adjust their styles more readily to fit the other person. And some people in your family will be more connected than others. Whatever the patterns, recognize that every interaction affects every family member either directly or indirectly.

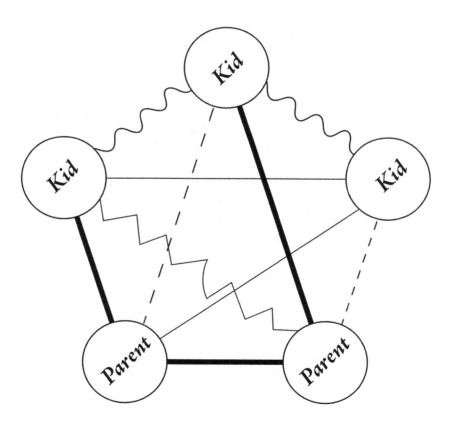

I'm always surprised by the far-reaching impact of even the smallest interactions in my own house. This is especially true in terms of the power I command with my mood. If I'm feeling happy, it'll trickle down quickly to my kids and husband. They'll magically respond to many situations that would otherwise provoke irritation with optimism instead. Unfortunately, the opposite is even more reliable.

If I allow interactions to be colored by my stress or annoyance, the shift for my family is nearly immediate. Three of the four other household members become equally crabby, while my middle son usually starts worrying and goes into "fixer" mode (unless his dad's or brothers' cascading grumpiness infects him first, in which case he's mostly just grumpy). Each of us then carries the weight of these feelings into the rest of our day and our other interactions. Whether we are unconsciously lifting or lowering the family vibe, it's clear that emotions are contagious.

The relationship web is always shape-shifting and evolving.

Day-to-day circumstances continually change the way people interact. Some events (family outings, time together, productive conversations) will strengthen connections, while others (arguments, traumas, unexpected setbacks, low-lying stressors) will compromise them. In the busy flow of life with young kids, the lines between caregivers might fade for a time only to be reinforced again whenever there's a need or opportunity for collaboration.

Despite the surface-level shifts, you're sure to find a more consistent blueprint underneath. Pull this deeper blueprint to the forefront. It will illuminate exchanges that shed light on more than just relationships between family members. It'll help you begin to see the functions those interactions have for the entire family as well.

HOW DO FAMILY DYNAMICS PLAY INTO GROWTH?

Zoom in momentarily on only the lines that reach your child. Make note of the "types" of lines reaching them. Which ones are consistent, strong, and supportive? Which ones are less so? Different interaction dynamics in a child's life are expected and desirable. Your child learns something different from each relationship, and every interaction provides a new opportunity to practice flexibility with their responses.

That's because the lines represent a two-way street, even for infants. We're wired from birth to take cues from even the most subtle feedback. Facial expressions, quality of eye contact, tone of voice, and body language all convey just as much—if not more—information than spoken words. Very young children read these cues and respond to them in their own way based on their previous learning and internal responses. The longer the feedback loop continues, the more they're learning.

As they grow, kids then begin observing and absorbing the other interactions occurring around them. The information gathering and eventual emulation of what they see isn't a conscious process, it's innate. Interaction patterns are often passed from parent to child outside of their conscious awareness. Often, the inheritance is multi-generational in depth and duration, imprinted and normalized over time.

Like any habit, you don't always realize it's happening—despite the significant impact it's having on you. Just as we tend to develop similar habits to the people around us, we tend to mirror the feelings and moods of the people in our inner circle. Mirror neurons are a specific class of sensory-motor cells in our brains that cause exactly that. They comprise the part of our neurology that enables us to learn through imitation.

These neurons operate not just by causing us to copy other people's actions, but also through triggering the expected feelings behind the actions as well. They enable us to reflect body language, facial expressions, and emotions. They play a big role in social learning. When you see someone smile, for example, your mirror neurons for smiling fire up too, creating a sensation in your mind of the feeling associated with smiling (i.e., happiness).

> *Because the scope of a child's world is mostly inside their home, so-cial-emotional and behavioral influences usually come from their immediate family.*

Parents, grandparents, and siblings model interactions in hundreds of small ways each day. Our kids learn from all of them, and the rest of the family is ultimately influenced each time as well. No two-way interaction occurs on its own, and family members are always impacted by the quality of each partnership.

WIDENING THE LENS

If your child is challenging you with difficult behaviors, step back and try to distance yourself from everything. Take advantage of your wider vantage point to see what's going on with the whole family. Larger-than-life power struggles, inability to focus on schoolwork, excessive sibling or peer conflict, anxiety, clinginess, rigidity, and big emotions that don't seem to match their circumstances are all examples. And each has roots in family conflict.

Behavior is tough to unpack, of course. It's possible that hard-to-manage behaviors are coming from a clinical concern or medical condition. Or that a mismatch of the physical environment with your child's internal state is causing them distress. Maybe it's a combination of things. But for now, try to leave other possible causes aside and look more closely at your family's relationship web (not the surface version—dig for the deeper blueprint).

This can be a complicated task while you're living inside the circumstances. It might help to enlist an outsider to puzzle out how communication and events within the family are influencing your child's behavior. A valuable third-party viewpoint can come from a trusted friend, extended family member, or professional.

The choice is yours, but no matter whom you involve, you'll need to keep an open mind. Let yourself absorb the feedback, even if it's not flattering. It'll help to acknowledge that all families experience ebbs and flows. Nobody is immune to life's difficulties.

> *Even the healthiest of relationships experience rough patches and have periods of necessary conflict.*

Conflict is uncomfortable, but it opens the door to insight, other perspectives, and possible solutions. The key is to maintain maturity and respect whenever you're working through disagreements or suggesting new ways of looking at things. Because the situation is already vulnerable, it can spiral quickly if some basic ground rules aren't in place. Don't lose sight of the big goal: the growth and wellness of your child and family.

TAKING ACTION

If you find that family dynamics are negatively impacting your child's behavior, the next thing to pay attention to is how much that can be mended. If your family is experiencing a trauma or stressor that is beyond your control, and if you're all already getting as much support as possible, you might just need to hold on until you come out the other side. But there could be some support you haven't yet tapped.

Support for your child can come in two ways: direct and indirect. Direct support is intervention geared specifically for and with your child. It might include consultations or direct visits with a therapist, teaching them new coping strategies, or just opening the door to a safe and meaningful conversation by explaining to them what's going on (in age-appropriate terms). Measurable relief can sometimes come from simple 10-minute bedtime talks with your child to help them unload thoughts, feelings, and unresolved misunderstandings.

Indirect support results from repairing relationships without your child's express involvement. Improving one-on-one dynamics within your family's web will benefit all members of your family, including your child. Healing is accomplished by doing the hard work of tackling any problems head-on (marital conflict, unmet needs, divergent goals, etc.) and improving the way the problems are aired at home during daily routines.

MANAGING SPECIFIC HARDSHIP

Sometimes the family's relationship web is negatively influenced not by a partnership conflict, but by one member's personal hardship or distress. When a disruption or trauma occurs, it affects everyone differently. The tragic loss that results from a miscarriage, for instance, impacts the mother who was carrying the child more intensely than it would the father or other siblings even though they, too, experience the loss.

Mom's healing period may be a time when she is less emotionally available to her partner and kids, which could be harder on them than the loss itself. The symptoms live in everyone, yet the source begins with one person's pain. In families, all emotions are shared.

Hardship affects one family member, and the relationship fallout is a consequence. The core issue doesn't live in the relationship; it lives in the individual and then has ripple effects in many places.

Through seeking help to work through a personal difficulty, an individual family member will ultimately benefit the whole family. No one is an island! Helping yourself and one another on the path to wellness will always serve to strengthen and elevate the wellness of your entire family unit.

Lucy, Nathan, and Emma were each under the age of 6 when their parents, Melissa and Gabe, began fighting more intensely. Melissa and Gabe's relationship had always been "bigger than life." Even so, they usually had an admirable way of transitioning from fighting to affection quickly. Then Gabe's baseline mood changed. He began showing symptoms of chronic stress that often expressed itself through anger.

Gabe was irritable and easy to provoke, and Melissa often responded by losing her patience with him. She had three kids to raise, after all. She didn't have the time, energy, or interest to indulge his mood swings.

But Gabe's irritability extended to the kids as well. Though they were young, they quickly learned to go quiet and withdraw at the first signs of annoyance from him. And when both parents went at it, it was all they could do to take cover. They learned quickly not to make waves. Anything could trigger their dad's anger, so they, like their mom, figured out how to keep the waters calm.

After a few months of this increased tension, the kids' everyday behavior changed in different ways. Lucy was becoming a "mother hen" and was preoccupied most of the time with fixing, pacifying, and making sure everything ran as smoothly as possible for everyone. She seemed older than her years, but she also started getting headaches and picking her nails until they bled.

Nathan was more withdrawn than ever and spent a lot of time lost in imaginative play alone in his bedroom. And Emma, the youngest, had become something of a wildling. She was nearly impossible to discipline and even harder to contain as she got into everything, seemingly without fear of consequences.

The changes were slow enough that Melissa didn't recognize them until her sister, who lived an hour away and didn't visit often, pointed them out to her. The tipping point came that afternoon when she heard Emma use, in context, an ugly phrase she must have overheard during an argument. Of course, Melissa knew that the fighting was impacting the kids, but she was rocked to her core by the thought that it could lead to unfortunate, lasting patterns of behavior.

Melissa knew that bringing her concern to Gabe would set him off, but she also knew it was important and that time was of the essence. She found a way to carefully deliver her concerns while they relaxed together on a Saturday morning. After seeing his impact on the kids in a new light, Gabe agreed to work with Melissa—over the course of several weeks—to better manage his stress. And just as important, they agreed to take a serious effort to temper each of their trigger responses in the heat of the moment.

Children are sometimes "symptom-carriers" for their parents. Typically, kids regress back to the most recent developmental acquisition when tension in the home rises. Often though, it isn't readily clear—especially when the parents don't recognize the connection between their actions and their kids' changes. A good rule of thumb is: Whenever tension becomes pervasive in the family, expect your kids to become temporarily less mature. That's how they cope.

MAKING IT STICK

Your long-term plan for healthy family dynamics will depend on the scope of any dysfunction you've been addressing. If a significant hardship or trauma has impacted your family, time and patience will continue to be your best remedy. Your usual support systems will help your efforts to be patient and allow time to heal.

> *Even when things are working fairly well, there will be occasions for tune-ups. In the hustle and bustle of life, there are surprisingly few moments when we feel like we have adequate breathing room to really connect, air grievances, and regroup with the people who matter most. Building a safe and productive sounding board into your family's routine is so valuable.*

There are many methods for accomplishing high-quality connections, depending on your circumstances. If your family enjoys predictable structure, one tried-and-true method is a regularly occurring family meeting. Coordinate a calendar time to all gather together (or, if it makes more sense, with adults only) to review everyone's satisfaction with the overall state of affairs.

But there are equally effective and much less formal ways. Take advantage of some naturally occurring opportunities to truly connect with one another. A minute here, a minute there can add up.

Go around the table during dinner (or lunch, or breakfast, or snack time) and ask everybody how their day was. You might not have everyone there, but it'll be time well spent even if it's just two of you. Have each person share at least one thing that's on their mind. Maybe have each family member name their best and worst part of the day. In my household, we call this routine "Best and Bummer," and we also tack on a compliment for someone else.

> *Put down or turn off technology, make eye contact, and really take in the person as they're speaking.*

Bedtime tuck-ins are another great opportunity for this. And sometimes the best moments happen in the car on the way to the next activity. This is especially true with older kids who are hard to pin down and might not feel comfortable with face-to-face conversation around tough topics.

The point is to make room for regular, genuine connection with all family members, even if only for brief periods. The busy pace of family life can chip away at our ability to connect and patch up relationship road bumps as they crop up. But if we're intentional about making space for our loved ones, the payoff is immeasurably valuable.

HOW WILL I KNOW ISSUES HAVE BEEN SUCCESSFULLY ADDRESSED?

The proof is in the pudding. You'll know you've succeeded in elevating your family dynamics if family members are feeling valued, seen, heard, and cared for. This doesn't mean that everything will be smooth sailing and there won't be disagreements, difficulty, or misfires in communication.

It would be highly suspicious if those things weren't a part of the fabric, even in a family with healthy dynamics. It's your response to the rough spots that matters. A family with good relationship dynamics stays attuned to one another's needs and can make adjustments whenever someone's emotional, physical, or mental wellness needs extra attention.

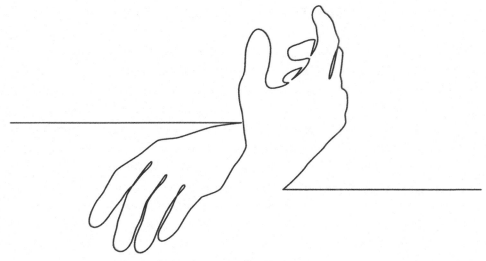

CHAPTER 5

YOUR NEEDS

IDENTIFYING THE IMPACT

This chapter is an extension of family dynamics, but with a narrowed focus. This is where we turn our attention to the specific needs of the primary caregiver. It's a universal truth that you need to put on your own oxygen mask before helping others. In families, this usually applies to parents. You can only provide full support and nurturing when you are having your own needs met first.

But to make that happen, you need to clarify exactly what your needs are. Some might be glaring, such as medical attention for a condition or illness and accessible childcare to attend to work or other responsibilities. But many needs—if not most—are far less visible.

A unique strain is placed on primary caregivers from the near-constant stream of demands that pour out of children. It's a 24-hour job unlike any other. Imagine you have an emotional bank account where both deposits and withdrawals happen around the clock. The weight of responsibility that you carry as the primary caregiver means there will always be a deficit between emotional deposits and emotional withdrawals. The role requires giving considerably more than taking.

As a result, two observations are important to note. First (and most obvious), a counterbalance must be built into your wellness plan. The absence of emotional deposits is unsustainable. This can take many forms and is usually best accomplished by answering the question, "If you could fill your free time (what free time?!) in any way, how would you spend that time?" Most parents' first reaction to this hypothetical is to name something they would do with their kids. But the secret answer is probably something done alone and that is recuperative.

The second observation is that the act of providing care is an emotional deposit. It feels good and nourishes the soul to deliver care. This intrinsic fuel, however, does not replace the need-meeting that comes from other more traditional recuperative sources.

> *The way we give care is also a message to the world about the way we would most like to receive care. Finding ways to be nurtured can refuel the spirit quite effectively. Who cares for the caregiver?*

GIVING 'TIL IT HURTS

In his 2013 book, *Give and Take*, Adam Grant reminds us of the crucial difference between "givers" who give at the expense of themselves and those who give from the platform of self-care. In short, those who only give through sacrificing their own needs eventually become depleted and are at risk of becoming "doormats."

The science is clear: the wellness of the primary caregiver is critical for sustainable and effective caregiving. Those who balance their own self-care with the delivery of care have a constantly replenishing reservoir of emotional energy and, in fact, receive unexpected support because of the goodwill they deliver to the world. People are happy to pay them back.

The problem is that the real world necessitates some imbalance now and again. Sometimes there just isn't enough time in the day to adequately meet everyone's needs, and the remaining deficit usually comes from the caregiver. Add in any extenuating circumstances—a child with medical or clinical needs, an aging parent who requires caregiving, work outside the home, or any of the million little fires that need putting out when you have a full life with children—and the scales will be tipped in disfavor of the one doing the caregiving.

WIDENING THE LENS

It's hard to be attentive to even some of your basic needs—balanced and regular meals, adequate sleep, and healthy routines—when pulled in too many directions. If your own essential needs aren't being met, your child is likely to be impacted by association.

> As the sidecar passenger in your everyday flow, your daily routines and habits will ultimately influence your child's daily routines and habits. We adopt the patterns, behaviors, and practices of those with whom we spend the most time. This is especially true for a young child who is an unwitting participant in their caregiver's schedule.

The unhealthy lifestyle that may result from your reduced self-care can lead to your child adopting a similarly unhealthy lifestyle.

Monkey see, monkey do. But fortunately, the mechanism works both ways. When you model good self-care and a healthy lifestyle, your child is equally primed and ready to imitate those things.

Each time you demonstrate sufficient attention to your own physical and emotional health, you're teaching the value of prioritizing good self-care habits. We all want our kids to be healthy in every way. Nothing is more powerful in getting that message across than striving to walk the walk and talk the talk yourself.

Unmet needs also influence your ability to give full attention to your child. We've all experienced being short-tempered with our loved ones when we're stressed, overtired, or feeling otherwise depleted and overwhelmed. Raise your hand if you've ever experienced being so mentally exhausted that all you want to do is mindlessly scroll through your phone while your kid is trying to interact with you.

Yes? Me, too. It's nearly impossible to be fully emotionally and cognitively attentive to anyone else when mile-long to-do lists, money troubles, overbooked schedules, health worries, or relationship problems are racing through your mind. When literal escapes aren't available, we find ways to create them through disengagement.

Your child could be feeling the brunt of that emotional fallout at times. Bad days are unavoidable, and they happen to the best of us. Kids are resilient and will weather random days when a caregiver is distracted, short-tempered, or emotionally unavailable. However, when those days begin to string together and form the baseline for the relationship, it's probably time for a reset.

TAKING ACTION

Take a mental inventory of all your needs that are not being satisfied. Think about current circumstances only. For example, if you've had periods of adequate childcare but today's needs have shifted for various reasons and you're feeling a stretch, then this is an area that needs attention.

Do some honest digging into the sources of stress in your life. Try to trace them back to specific elements within your day-to-day flow. Your answers might be centered in schedule-based imbalances, logistical holes, or relationship-centered breaches, or they might include a little bit of everything.

Recognize that leaving any of your needs unmet will create a source of stress in your day. Stress triggers and stress responses don't follow a formula. What might not bother one person can feel like an all-consuming burden to another.

> *Everyone has a unique set of needs. Understanding and respecting your individual stress triggers and responses is key to making an effective plan. Knowing yourself helps you know your child. Your stressors are delivered to them, as is your ability to achieve a sense of calm.*

You'll also need to figure out how much you're able to influence the impact of the stress. Many of life's stressors are here to stay. Rather than focus on their removal, you might want to put your energy into lessening the consequences. Doing so will still go a long way in helping to soften the repercussions of stress on you and, by extension, your child. Here are a few ideas:

- ✦ If the unmet needs are schedule-based, evaluate how much flexibility you have in reducing the strain by limiting activities, simplifying responsibilities, or tapping your wider circle for assistance (outsource rides, delegate responsibilities).
- ✦ If the needs are logistical (the family car isn't available when

needed, there's a childcare gap, the home or neighborhood environment isn't supporting your child's growing requirements), take a deeper look at what adjustments can be made using an honest analysis of the family's resources. See if people, money, and objects can be reallocated in more helpful ways.

♦   If the stressors are stemming from relationship-centered breaches, it's time to have a conversation about what might be done to begin the process of interpersonal repair. As I mentioned before, this chapter is tied closely to the Family Dynamics chapter.

ONE FOR ALL, ALL FOR ONE?

Western culture doesn't support a whole lot of caring for the caregiver these days. Nuclear families are busier and more isolated than ever. Multi-generational households are becoming scarce, and there's a growing expectation that caregivers should handle child-rearing responsibilities by themselves.

Living the "It takes a village to raise a child" philosophy can feel like a constant uphill battle fraught with resistance. Staying in the battle is worthwhile, but it's hard to do when you're already feeling worn down and your environment doesn't support the cause. So, who comprises your "village"?

Sometimes it helps to redefine the way we think about the "village" in today's context. The help that you may have gotten from extended family might now be in the hands of others. Perhaps your child's teacher, daycare provider, pediatrician, speech and language therapist, social worker, occupational therapist, or others are now in the spectrum of helpers in your community.

Beyond professional services, these teammates offer respite and alternative perspectives when a parent feels depleted or stuck. Even a brief conversation with someone you trust and respect can recharge the batteries and shed light on new ways to look at parenting challenges. Defining the inhabitants of your "village" is essential.

G illian felt foggy right after waking up in the morning. She noticed she was fumbling on tasks that should have been second nature, such as putting her client's sessions into her calendar as soon as they were scheduled and making sure she had enough breast milk stored to leave with her parents while she was at work. Admittedly, sometimes her mistakes were amusing, like the day she put her hairdryer away in the refrigerator. But it wasn't nearly as amusing to realize she flaked out on a client or her daughter didn't have a bottle after her nap.

As a social worker, mom of two young kids, and the primary household manager, she was running on empty most of the time. The family/house workload used to be more equitable between her wife and herself, but the bulk had slowly shifted to her when they had their second baby and she was home more of the time. Now that she was working professionally a little bit again, she was still somehow responsible for the lion's share. She told herself it was easier to take care of everything herself than to have to coach someone else through it—and anyway, wasn't this phase of life supposed to be draining? Everyone said so.

Her parents were doing the babysitting, which was a tremendous help. Unfortunately, given the day-to-day unpredictability of her schedule coupled with her parents' busy lives, they weren't always reliable or punctual. They also did exactly what grandparents should do, which was to enjoy her kids and spend all of their time together having fun—but that meant she usually had a big clean-up job afterward on top of her usual marathon of chores.

Most of the overwhelming minutiae of Gillian's day was off her wife's radar. Her wife wanted to be helpful, but she left for work just as the kids were stirring and didn't come home until their bedtime. She also had a gift for somehow sleeping right through all of the middle-of-the-night feedings and preschooler bathroom trips. Gillian knew there was room for improvement in the balancing of responsibilities, but their system had become normalized, and...well, she had gotten used to it.

Then Gillian became sick and couldn't seem to get better. Her seasonal cold turned into bronchitis, and after weeks of exhaustion, she went to her doctor. Aside from the usual treatment, his recommended remedy was direct and clear: Slow down. Sleep more. Take better care of yourself.

Empowered by her doctor's "prescription," she approached her wife about making changes. Her wife agreed to do some of the nighttime parenting and work out a better plan for household chores. They also arranged to reallocate some of their income for a paid babysitter to come in one day per week so Gillian would have a consistent block of time to do her work and run errands.

The improvement was nearly instantaneous. While daily life was still hectic and far from stress-free, Gillian felt a significant weight lift from her shoulders. It was amazing what a little extra free time, slightly better sleep, and the promise of more reliable support was able to do for her health and spirits.

The kids seemed to notice, too. Her preschooler reveled in Gillian's increased availability and regularly woke up talking about his plans for whatever pretend-play scheme they could enact together that day. And the toddler was delighted with their new routine of spending a bit of daily unstructured one-on-one time together—time that Gillian would have normally spent running through her to-do list.

Even her wife's mood seemed brighter. Gillian realized her physical and emotional state set the trend for the rest of the family. Helping herself had helped all of them. Now, the trick would be to sustain the change. Things have a way of slipping back, and this self-care and rebalancing lesson would need to last.

MAKING IT STICK

As you make plans to better meet your needs, work together with other members of your family to establish the long-term benefits. Some of the changes you've identified as worthwhile might, in fact, increase family stress levels by temporarily disrupting some of your established patterns. Attending to your own needs (reallocating family funds, digging into relationship problems, beginning or altering therapy services, overhauling your child's childcare situation, or even changing their school) can provide the course-correction that turns the corner.

Be patient. Although changes might be hard on everyone up front, they can represent an enormous investment in your emotional and physical well-being—and ultimately, that of the whole family. The pain of change is eventually rewarded.

Positive change frequently begins with an element of difficulty and upheaval, but the dust will eventually settle, I promise. And once it does, you'll probably wonder why you didn't go to the trouble sooner. Keep this reassurance in mind as you continue to tackle any longer-term alterations because it's vital that everyone stays on the same page to make the change last.

As the person on the front lines of your child's developmental support system, you function as the primary gatekeeper, architect, administrator, and teacher in your child's world. Weathering the process of improving your own circumstances will reap big benefits for your child. So, how do you know if your course corrections were the right moves if the evidence doesn't unfold until later?

HOW WILL I KNOW ISSUES HAVE BEEN SUCCESSFULLY ADDRESSED?

Here's one way to find out if your needs are being met effectively: do some self-reflection. Are there still some areas for improvement? If so, how can they be addressed more efficiently or effectively? After making some changes, does it feel like things in your day are running more smoothly, and have you experienced an improvement in the quality of time spent with your child?

Of course, natural caregivers tend to minimize the impact of stress. "I'm fine" is a common reply to "Are you OK?" Push your response beyond the automatic follow-up to "How are you?"

The "I'm fine" reply is often an attempt to move the conversation past the genuine concern motivating the question. Share your real feelings about circumstances. And if you're the one doing the asking, help the recipient understand that you truly want to know how they are doing—even if that means hearing a difficult answer.

After any changes have had some time to take effect, do an informal pre/post comparison. Even if you aren't exactly where you hope to end up, celebrate any comparative upward movement you've experienced. Keep in mind that the groundwork you've laid will likely have continual benefits, at each stage of development.

CHAPTER 6

YOUR CHILD'S DEVELOPMENTAL STAGE

IDENTIFYING THE IMPACT

Whether responding to a trauma or seizing an opportunity, developmental timing is key. It's clear that the same family disruption or environmental opportunity will affect a 1-year-old, 6-year-old, and 11-year-old differently. It's also important to understand that no two 1-year-olds, 6-year-olds, or 11-year-olds are ever operating from precisely the same developmental stage.

Developmental stages are marked by the various physical, social-emotional, and intellectual phases that a child experiences as they mature. The usual stair-step stages of development we see in books, online, and at the pediatrician's office are a useful way to track children's growth and readiness for learning. The benchmarks give us an idea of when certain needs, behaviors, and experiences are common.

That knowledge can help prepare us to make the most of our children's innate potential. But it's important to keep in mind that the frameworks are largely theoretical and never, ever one-size-fits-all. We'll begin by taking a quick look at the science.

There are many variations on developmental stages out there, but for our purposes, we will draw from Jean Piaget's theory of cognitive development, Erik Erikson's stages of psychosocial development, and traditional motor development theory. Let's first review each theory briefly.

Cognitive development theory (Piaget) describes the interaction between the environment and the in-born capacities of a child. As they acquire knowledge, the child develops a scaffolded understanding of the world. The theory has four stages:

Sensorimotor stage (infancy)	Babies learn about the world through their senses and through their actions (moving around and exploring their environment).
Preoperational stage (toddlerhood and preschool years)	Toddlers and young children acquire the ability to internally represent the world through language and mental imagery.
Concrete operational stage (elementary school years)	Children begin thinking logically about concrete events. They become less egocentric and begin to think about how other people might think and feel.
Formal operational stage (adolescence)	Adolescents learn to deal with abstract ideas and consider hypothetical problems with many possible solutions.

Psychosocial development theory (Erikson) combines biological, psychological, and social factors on growth, and each stage has two dichotomous outcomes. Every outcome builds upon the others, so they either contribute to or impede the stages that follow. The theory has eight stages in total, but we'll narrow our focus to the five that typically occur during childhood:

Trust vs. mistrust (infancy)	Babies depend on caregivers, usually parents, for their basic needs. They learn to trust others based on how well caregivers meet their needs.
Autonomy vs. shame and self-doubt (toddlerhood)	Young children begin exploring the world around them. They learn more about their environment and their place within it while developing basic skills.
Initiative vs. guilt (preschool years)	Preschoolers become increasingly focused on doing things themselves and establishing their own goals.
Industry vs. inferiority (early school years)	As children grow in independence, they become increasingly aware of themselves as individuals. They begin to compare themselves with others.
Identity vs. role confusion (adolescence)	During this stage, adolescents' main goal is to answer the question "Who am I?" They may try on different personas to determine which roles fit them best.

Motor development theory tells us that motoric development progresses through six broad stages during a child's life:

Reflexive	Inborn neurological responses
Rudimentary	Early purposeful movement
Fundamental	Basic movement skills
Sports skill	Complex movement skills
Growth and refinement	Advanced skills
Peak performance	Mastery

Motor development is age-related, but it's not age-dependent. Although there are typical periods in which they occur, they can happen at any time within a person's life. Some people will hit all of the stages, and some won't.

Even when a person achieves all six stages, it is likely to be only within a very specific skill set. The ranges of typical motor acquisition and mastery are fairly wide. They are impacted by personality and interests, biological predisposition, disability, and absence or presence of environmental supports. So, let's broaden our focus to the common themes of these theories.

BOILING IT ALL DOWN

The particulars of these models don't matter nearly as much as your understanding of where your child is currently operating within the three broad universal stages: cognitive (*intellectual*), psychosocial (*emotional/behavioral*), and motor (*physical*) development. If you're feeling unsure, check in with your trusted circle or reach out to new professionals who can help assess your child. Other family members, daycare providers, teachers, pediatricians, and pediatric support professionals can offer valuable perspectives on your child's developmental stage based on observations of your child within their settings.

> *Beware of the trap of Googling the information or relying on so-cial media platforms. While these sources provide access to credi-ble information, they also lead to misinformation, as they are not rigorously vetted. When it comes to your child, your trusted circle of friends, family, and professionals is the most reliable source of support.*

WIDENING THE LENS

Once you feel like you have a fairly good idea of your child's current developmental stage, it's time to figure out how it's contributing to your child's involvement in the events of their day. It will also help you see how your child is likely to respond to changes you'd like to make.

One of the hardest aspects of this is that your child is constantly growing. If you're lucky, you can celebrate a win for a nanosecond. There are so many examples of small victories: settling into a pretty good sleep schedule after weeks of struggle, getting your child to try something new following resistance, or finding the one item (blankie, pacifier, teddy bear, fidget gadget) that reliably soothes them. Anchor these gains before the ground suddenly shifts under you once again.

Parenting is a constant exercise in adaptability. It can feel like you're always playing catch-up, and in many respects, you are. Em-brace the notion of continuous change. It is the fuel for development.

Although it's nice to catch your breath during developmental pla-teaus, remember that these rest periods are simply the child's way of preparing for the next stage of growth. In fact, oftentimes the plateaus are the signal that a change is about to occur.

Early in my own parenting journey, I noticed that my son had a few days of being more irritable right before some new ability would break through. After days of struggling to express what he was feeling, for instance, the words suddenly flowed out of him. It seemed that I was always being alerted to an impending stage of growth, yet I often didn't recognize the behavioral clues until after the fact.

> *There isn't a parenting expert out there who hasn't felt personally bewildered at some point by their own child morphing before their eyes.*

Be heartened by the knowledge that everyone struggles to keep up. You're in good company. Even as an author of a parenting book and a parent of three children, I often have moments when I don't know what to do.

Your child will keep you on your toes, but as long as you're focusing on the broad strokes of where they are in the developmental timeline, you're doing fine. Recognize that we all lack confidence, especially in situations we've never faced.

ARE THERE ANY INTERVENING VARIABLES?

It's important to take note of any extenuating circumstances affecting your child's development. Physical disabilities, learning disabilities, and other special needs (such as a sensory processing disorder or an emotional or behavioral disorder) can disrupt the course of growth. A trauma that your child is experiencing, or one that involves the family as a whole, can also modify the expression of skills.

These variables are significant enough to alter your child's developmental trajectory in one way or another. Of course, the extent of that influence will be another moving target for you to track. Remember, developmental stages don't have firm beginning and ending ages, despite what the magazine articles might argue.

Timing of growth hinges on your child's disposition, your child's innate abilities, and your family's response. It will also depend on the demands of the task or environment. Certain variables might not pose a problem in most settings or during some stretches of time, only to become amplified later.

This is why we need to stay nimble and watch for changes, and also why we need to give ourselves grace whenever we miss things at first glance. Norms are for textbooks. Actual developmental acquisition happens in its own time.

TAKING ACTION

Daniel Winnicott's "good enough" parenting concept (Guide to Psychoanalytic Developmental Theories, 2009) is a useful guide for providing flexible support while our kids develop. A fail-safe way to facilitate children's growth and learning is by simply creating a nurturing environment that harnesses their developmental potential. If nothing else, Winnicott recommends providing these three things:

1. Unconditional acceptance, caring, and commitment:
    *   Establish trust.
    *   Build a foundation for future attachments.
2. Consistent limit setting:
    *   Create boundaries in the absence of internal control.
    *   Help kids internalize the ability to self-soothe.
3. Facilitation of development:
    *   Be alert to the timing of natural learning opportunities.
    *   There's no need to push—move with the flow of the child's unique path.

How you finesse each of these depends on the understanding of your child's capabilities and their current cognitive, psychosocial, and motor development. But the intention remains the same throughout all of the stages. It comes down to providing a flexible framework of expectation along with consistent understanding and support. Raising the bar in response to growth works most powerfully when it happens in the form of gentle, encouraging nudges coupled with open arms to fall into when your child stumbles.

Sometimes, you might even allow your child to fall without a catch if the lesson teaches them how to land or how to get back up (recall my lesson from teaching my oldest son how to ride a bike). The social and physical environment plays a big role in conveying whether to position yourself for the catch or the fall. Messages and lessons from caregivers come in many forms (e.g., letting go might better support their growth than holding on).

The messages and lessons are delivered in the words you choose, the tone you use, and the grace you give when mistakes are made and slips occur (for both your child and yourself). They're in the adjustments you make in response to what your child is showing you. They're in the way you set up the physical space and your child's experiences within it: objects, cues for action, barriers, and access.

Children learn by watching you and reading the environment. Growth is the result of a never-ending process of acting on your surroundings and making note of the impact of your responses.

Your child is making constant adjustments and recalibrating their understanding based on how the world reacts to them. This action-re-action-readjustment routine is a lifelong occupation. (It's the way you learn to parent as well!) It's a self-reinforcing spiral when you pay attention to the subtle exchanges.

CHAPTER 6: YOUR CHILD'S DEVELOPMENTAL STAGE

Every child has a different way of perceiving, processing, and integrating environmental input. Part of it develops in the womb and is fundamental to the child's make-up. The other part is a byproduct of their developmental stage, which is why it's so important to take environmental input into account when determining actions to improve growth, learning, and behavior.

Something was going on with Aliyah, but her parents couldn't put their finger on what. She had always been a little intense. They usually interpreted her intensity as persistence.

When she was a baby, she'd watched her parents carefully, and they delighted in seeing her little face try to mimic their expressions. During her toddler and preschool years, she frequently zeroed in on her brother, parents, or grandmother when engaged in a task. Before long, they'd catch her trying out the same thing on her own until she had mastered it. When she was 2, she once calmly sat with her brother's action figures for 15 minutes trying to keep them from falling off the seats in their jeep before they could "drive" away. They marveled at her determination.

Now that she was in first grade, her fortitude seemed to plunge off a cliff. She became discouraged by nearly everything. Her family grew accustomed to hearing her roar with frustration when doing her schoolwork, being asked to help around the house, or any time something didn't go her way.

All Aliyah wanted to do was play with her toys and color pictures. Even playdates with good friends went south more often than not. The adults in the family found themselves managing Aliyah's temper no matter what was happening.

There was nothing different at home to help them pinpoint the root of the problem. Her teacher also had a hard time explaining the shift. Aliyah's parents tried giving her an earlier bedtime, and although Aliyah relented after some initial protesting, the extra sleep didn't seem to help much.

In fact, she seemed to be sleeping more fitfully than ever. Her mom wondered if anxiety was the culprit, but talking to her about things during calmer moments didn't reveal anything significant. Everyone had a different notion of how to respond. In the end, her grandmother had it right: "Leave her be. She's growing."

Following a few weeks of enduring "Aliyah the Tornado," her family woke up one Sunday morning to a pleasant surprise. Aliyah seemed like a different child altogether. She was agreeable and even jovial at moments during breakfast.

Wanting to capitalize on her good mood (and the resulting happy vibe of the whole family at the table), they sat around to have a long conversation. They noticed Aliyah was using a more expanded vocabulary than usual and making unexpected connections. She understood jokes that they assumed would go over her head, and shared insights that astonished them about what she was hearing.

Her grandmother had nailed it. The angst was just the symptom of a developmental growth spurt. She had seen this a few times before while raising Aliyah's mother.

It might not have been observable to an outsider, but the transformation in Aliyah was palpable to her immediate family. Their little girl seemed to have matured overnight. After some reflection, they knew better.

She'd been busy working on a cognitive burst while her behavior seemed to deteriorate. It was clear now she had been funneling her energy into "growing her brain" and developing *new critical thinking skills. Her ability to manage emotion and behavior had been sidelined so she could focus on working out her novel abilities.*

MAKING IT STICK

This is an area where frequent check-ins for accuracy are important. Kids grow at unpredictable speeds and in variable ways. New skill integration happens differently for each child and at different times.

Sometimes growth comes in stops and starts. It may take the form of a burst. Other times it happens steadily and gradually, and nearly under the radar. If we're not paying attention, transitions may catch us off guard.

A formal assessment usually isn't needed to figure out if your child has entered a new stage of development. An obvious new skill, a different behavior, or an unexpected response will usually signal a developmental transition. There may be other times when you can sense something has shifted but you can't quite put your finger on it.

When this happens, step back and try to paint a bigger picture of how your child today compares with the version of your child you observed last season, last month, and even last week. Development has a knack for occurring outside our consciousness at the same time that it's right under our noses. It's easy to take growth for granted when you see your child every day.

Sustaining change boils down to how well the new expectations are matching up with your child's ability. You don't need to have exact developmental age ranges scored on a skills checklist to know if your child is grooving with circumstances or faltering in some way. While it's true that faltering might be a result of some other factor (or a combination of a few), make sure you consider the impact of any new developmental shifts.

And if something doesn't seem to be gelling for an extended period, there's no harm in calling for reinforcements. Think about the professionals in your network. Whose voices are you needing to hear? Which community partners best support your goals for this phase of your child's growth?

Teachers, care providers, and therapists (occupational, speech, physical, developmental, and social/psychological) are all equipped to provide a window into current developmental levels of functioning. Asking for help or simply a fresh perspective from a trained professional does not mean there is something wrong with your child. Experts live among us, and they are eager to be on your team.

Tapping their insights only expands the pool of resources to consider when you're trying to figure out what is happening, why it's happening, and what to do next (if anything). Outside perspectives often teach us that "normal development" is rarely "normal." The mean is simply an average from a pool of data that represents a wide range of growth.

HOW WILL I KNOW ISSUES HAVE BEEN SUCCESSFULLY ADDRESSED?

Not all areas of development (intellectual, emotional/behavioral, physical) progress in unison. One area of development might take a backseat—or even appear to undergo regression—for energy to be funneled into another area for a while. Each kid's natural aptitudes will also serve to strengthen some skills more while other areas always seem to lag a little.

For example, some kids are naturally attuned to emotions and will spend every opportunity developing rich pretend play. Even though they might have little intrinsic drive to work on motor skills, their creative powers are on fire. While you are concerned about progress in one area, another area is soaring.

CHAPTER 6: YOUR CHILD'S DEVELOPMENTAL STAGE

You know your child best. You'll know you've been successful in understanding and incorporating your child's stage of development if these two things are generally true:

1. Your child is making progress following their usual (and perfectly unique-to-them) trajectory.
2. You've found ways to shape your child's experiences to build on natural strengths and support areas for growth.

After any tweaks you've made have had time to take effect, do an informal pre/post comparison to further gauge success. Note any changes. As with all the other areas, it's unrealistic to expect success all of the time, especially with the unpredictability of kids' maturation. Striving for any upward movement is still a worthy goal.

Recall that scoring on a scale (like the method used in the Family Environmental Assessment Tool) can be subjective by design. Unlike a grading scale where performance is built into the choices, the F.E.A.T. scale captures a baseline moment in time from which to compare future progression or regression. What happens next is what counts. Has the issue being evaluated improved or deteriorated since the last measurement?

Why do you think that is? Was the movement due to something you did or didn't do? Was it just a consequence of growth? Did the environment shift in a way that impacted your family?

These are the types of questions the informal comparison is meant to trigger. The conversations that follow will shepherd the direction and pace of growth. Of course, there will always be enablers and obstacles. Let's give thought to the factors that propel or inhibit normal development.

CHAPTER 7

YOUR ENABLERS & OBSTACLES

IDENTIFYING THE IMPACT

In this chapter, we'll discuss things that come to mind when you consider the question, "What actually makes up my kid's world?" This is where we dig into the elements of your child's physical spaces, the objects that surround them, their activities, the peers they regularly encounter, and the resources that they have available to them.

We're all deeply influenced by our surroundings, probably much more than we realize. From the moment you open your eyes in the morning to when your head hits the pillow at night, you're barraged by literally thousands of interactions with various items, people, and structures that color your experiences, shape your movements, and inform your decisions. It would be impossible to list them all.

Many of the influences in our surroundings become invisible because they're always there. Over time, the "normalization" phenome-non numbs us to their presence and impact. To perceive them, you'd have to try to adopt the wide-eyed innocence of a child, as though it was the first time you had ever noticed something.

> *As adults, we've become immune to most of the daily influx. But to children, it's a nearly non-stop cascade of environmental sig-nals for engagement and behavior. Young children don't have the depth of experience that we, or even older children, do when it comes to filtering the usefulness of environmental enablers and obstacles.*

Kids simply respond to influences and learn from the experience. Not only has their environment not been normalized, but everything is new! Imagine what your day would be like if everything was be-ing experienced for the first time. It would probably be some blend of amazement and the labor of having to process new information constantly.

We can see this clearly in toddlers' behavior. Once they're able to begin moving and acting on their environment, toddlers tend to be busy explorers (until they crash). Of course, every child is unique, and some are more cautious and less prone to exploration than others.

But aside from personality differences, they're all driven by a sense of curiosity and investigation. It's wired into their system so they can build a foundation of knowledge about their world. Think of your child as a little scientist; every action and reaction in their day is a mini-experiment designed to gain information about their own capacities and how they fit with the surroundings.

If an interaction with an object, person, or structure is successful and brings positive results and feelings, your child is likely to try it again. Of course, the reverse is also true. If an interaction is unsuccessful or brings negative results and feelings, they may try a few more times (depending on individual disposition), but they'll be prone to eventually avoid or dismiss it in the future.

Learning is constant at this stage of life while the brain is still developing. Neuroscience experts tell us that the brain grows and changes at a rapid pace for the first 25 years of our lives. Neuroplasticity continues to alter our capacity after childhood, but those first few years are important.

Imagine a squeezed sponge at the edge of a puddle of water. As you release the sponge, it quickly absorbs whatever is in the puddle. As a parent, it is your job to guide what's in the puddle.

Some of those ingredients propel growth while others hinder. Just because they hinder doesn't mean they're not valuable. We learn a lot when we figure out how to navigate an obstacle. Experiences of accomplishment and frustration both move kids forward.

FIGHTING THE GOOD FIGHT

Technology is a stand-out example of just how quickly a rewarding experience can drive a child to "try again" and seek more of the same. There's a booming industry that has the sole purpose of wielding psychological principles to make products and services more enticing and keep us engaged. It's based on an addiction model. Modern techniques are scarily impressive in their ability to draw us in and sink their teeth in.

YouTube, tablet and phone applications, and all other forms of media—whether passive or interactive—are carefully designed to hook us through a satisfying multisensory experience. Even though the rewards are often brief and shallow, they tend to come quickly and intensely. Reward centers in the brain are fired up again and again.

The result is that they leave us wanting more.

Media offers a clear illustration of how intentional design can elicit feedback loops to shape behavior, but there are so many other powerful influences integrated into the scenery. The concept is nothing new. Our shopping habits, the activities we choose to spend our time on, the objects we value, and even the types of relationships we seek and work to maintain are byproducts of emotional feedback loops.

Taking an inventory of the environmental messages that your child regularly encounters throughout the day is an eye-opening exercise. Some parts of your family's and child's environment are fundamentally unchangeable. However, you're sure to find a sizable portion that can be crafted with intention. You might be surprised by the extent of sway you have over much of it, particularly within your home.

WIDENING THE LENS

Try listing the environmental factors (structures, items, and interpersonal interactions) that seem to be consistent in your child's day. Just to start the ball rolling, go for the big players first (people, activities, locations) and see what else comes once you get a little momentum. Next, try to divide your list into two general categories: helpful (*enablers*) or unhelpful (*obstacles*).

This exercise can be performed in a couple of ways. One is to go to a "panoramic view" and think generally about the way your child moves through their day. This is a valuable undertaking. Even the parts of the schedule that seem to be going well probably have some elements that are ripe for improvement. Another approach is to zoom in on a specific problem area in your child's life.

Let's go through an example. Imagine that persuading your child to do schoolwork is the bane of your parenting existence, and you'd like to take immediate action to fix that. Begin by narrowing your focus to only the environmental enablers (helpful things) and obstacles (unhelpful things) that contribute to schoolwork time.

List as many as you can on a notepad. Just remember that there may be things affecting your child that aren't obvious parts of the immediate scene. In the same way that earlier snacking ruins later appetite, there may be environmental influences that are sabotaging your child's focus and engagement when it's time to sit down. Try to broaden the context to more than just the fixed time your child is expected to be working to pinpoint those sneaky before-and-after influences.

Enablers:

- Kid-friendly desk/chair
- Plenty of school supplies
- Strong internet (when working)
- Eats beforehand (shouldn't be hungry)
- Has some downtime first (well rested)
- Brother working nearby (motivation/camraderie)
- Dad usually available to help

Obstacles:

- Toys/fidgets on desk
- Too many supplies/mess
- Internet goes out a lot
- Sugar crash!
- Plays on tablet beforehand (hates stopping)
- Brother working nearby (distraction/comparison)
- Mom working nearby (audible)
- Tired (swim lessons go late)
- Backlog of assignments (overwhelming)

You're bound to encounter items that beg for placement in both columns. When this happens, you may want to delineate the item by looking at the specific times and contexts of its influence. For instance, if a kid-height snack station exists in your kitchen, there will be times when it's appropriate for your child to practice independence by getting their own snacks.

On the other hand, full access to unlimited goodies right before a meal or unlimited access throughout the day so your child has no appetite for dinner isn't quite as helpful. This structural factor (your kid-accessible snack cabinet) would then appear in both columns, but under different parameters. Remember to look at this from a variety of perspectives.

PLAYING DETECTIVE

Some of your conclusions will be based on guesswork. You'll need to put on several hats all at once for this: psychologist/scientist/anthropologist/scene investigator. If you're uncertain how to begin, start simply by looking at your child's immediate physical space. Evaluate how its components are either helping or hindering behavior.

- Does your child have the right tools for the job they're expected to do?
- Are they distracted by too many toys or unrelated environmental stimuli (noise, activity level, etc.)?
- Do their playing and learning spaces provide the right signals for the desired goal?
- Is your child being given enough time to follow through on things?
- Is support available when needed?

When you're ready to zoom out a little, give thought to some of the overarching influences on your child's learning and behavior. One component to consider is your child's activity schedule. Every child has an innate sweet spot when it comes to activity level. Introversion/

extroversion plays a big role here, as does the type of activities in their day. Some activities will be draining for your child, while others will energize them.

> *The trend these days is to begin enrichment and sports activities at an early age, under the precept that "more is better." This is great for some kids, while others require more downtime to refuel and synthesize all of the information they've been asked to absorb. It's rare for a child to recognize they're feeling overbooked, and rarer still that they'll find the words to tell you so.*

Your child is likely to show you they're feeling overwrought through behavioral clues. Fatigue, irritability, anxiety, and even aggression are all signals of being overwhelmed. For kids who display these things regularly, it might be better to adopt a "less is more" approach.

Peer influence is another environmental component that can be easily overlooked or underestimated. Your child develops an understanding about which behaviors are acceptable, which interests are valued, and which aspects of performance are esteemed by observing others. This usually begins with the adults in their lives, but as they age, the scales eventually tip toward the other children in their day.

Siblings and regularly present peers, including cousins, classmates, and neighborhood friends, can have a significant influence, each in a different way. Siblings and cousins inherit the credibility of family. Classmates share daily common experiences. Neighborhood friends become the playmates, and exploration and discovery unfold.

By extension, your child's birth order also bears consideration. While birth order theories (like the one that follows) can feel overly simplistic, there are inevitably some kernels of truth in them. Your parenting style is built upon past experience, and it continues to evolve as you gain insight. Parents learn right alongside their children.

No one enters the parenting journey with a proven playbook. If you have multiple children, you're using trial-and-error learning with each kid's personality as you go—regardless of how equitable you aim to be. And if you have one child, your energy and focus are bound to be different than if other kids were in the mix. Those differences serve to set the stage uniquely for each child.

ADLERIAN OVERVIEW OF BIRTH ORDER CHARACTERISTICS
(This is a broad simplification of Adler's theory.)

POSITION	FAMILY SITUATION	CHILD'S CHARACTERISTICS
ONLY	Birth is a miracle. Parents have no previous experience and may be timid or anxious. Retains 200% attention from both parents through childhood. Matures early.	Can be overprotected and spoiled. Likes being the center of attention. Often has difficulty sharing. Prefers adult company and uses adult language. Disappointed if abilities aren't promptly recognized and rewarded. May be socially inept with peers.
OLDEST	Dethroned by the next child; feels loss of power and control. Must learn to share. Parent expectations are usually very high. Often given extra responsibility and expected to set an example.	Feels power is their right and strives to gain it back. Overemphasizes the importance of authority, rules, laws. May become authoritarian or strict. Many are "problem" kids but can become helpful if encouraged. Often focused on the past and pessimistic about the future.
SECOND	Parents ease up and tend to demand or expect less. Has a pacesetter in the older sibling, who may be seen as a model or a threat. Language and motor skills develop faster than the older child.	Is competitive and ambitious. Sets high goals. May become a rebel or try to outdo everyone. Competition can deteriorate into rivalry. Can be more successful or talented than an older sibling but may give up if the oldest consistently excels. Often more optimistic than older sibling.
MIDDLE	Is "sandwiched" in. May feel squeezed out of a position of privilege and significance. Always has to share and never gets first pick.	May be even-tempered, with a "take it or leave it" attitude. May have trouble with setting or reaching goals or finding a place in the world. May become a fighter of injustice.

YOUNGEST	Has many mothers and fathers. Older children try to educate them. Never dethroned, but never experiences real power either. Often spoiled or pampered by parents and siblings.	Wants to be bigger than the others. Highly motivated to excel but often sets unrealistic goals. Has huge plans that never seem to work out. Because of the desire to succeed in everything, never develops one central ambition. A dreamer. Has trouble establishing independence. May be helpless under pressure and may have a good deal of unrealized potential.
TWIN	One is usually stronger or more active. Parents may see one as older or more mature.	Can have identity problems. Strives to separate self from other, to be independent. May lack direction or be a follower. Stronger one may become the leader.
"GHOST CHILD"	Child born after the death of the first child may have a "ghost" in front of him. Mother may become overprotective.	Child may exploit a mother's over-concern for their well-being, or may rebel and protest the feeling of being compared to an idealized memory. Struggles to be their own person.
ADOPTED CHILD	Parents may be so thankful to have a child that they spoil them. They may try to compensate for the loss of the child's biological parents.	Child may become very spoiled and demanding. Child may come to resent the adoptive parents and idealize the biological parents, or child may resent perceived abandonment by biological parents and strive to feel worthy of love.
ONLY BOY AMONG GIRLS	Usually with women all the time, if father is away.	May try to prove he is the man in the family and develop hyper-masculine characteristics, or may become effeminate.
ONLY GIRL AMONG BOYS	Older brothers may act as her protectors. May try to please the father.	Can become very feminine, dependent, and helpless. Or may become a tomboy and try to outdo the brothers.
ALL BOYS	If a mother wanted a girl, can be dressed or treated as a girl.	Child may capitalize on an assigned role or protest it vigorously.
ALL GIRLS	May be dressed or treated as a boy.	Child may capitalize on an assigned role or protest it vigorously.

Adler's Notes

1. The psychological situation of each child in the family is different.

2. The child's **opinion** of themselves and their situation determines his choice of attitude.

3. If more than three years separate children, sub-groups of birth order may form.

4. A child's birth order position may be seized by another child if circumstances permit (e.g., sibling's illness or weakness; parents' treatment differs from expectations).

5. Competition may be expressed in choice of interests or development of personality characteristics.

6. Birth order is sometimes not a major influence on personality development. The other potentially significant influences are parental attitudes, social and economic position, and gender roles.

7. Adler speculated that birth order differences would begin to disappear when families became less competitive and autocratic, and more cooperative and democratic.

   Adapted from Henry T. Stein, Ph.D., and Duane Schultz, Ph.D. For more comprehensive information about birth order, read: *What Life Could Mean to You*, by Alfred Adler; *The Individual Psychology of Alfred Adler*, edited by Heinz and Rowena Ansbacher; and *The Collected Works of Lydia Sicher: An Adlerian Perspective*, edited by Adele Davidson.

TAKING ACTION

Adults can only monitor and curate so much. You may have carefully selected the music playing in the car to be educational and age-appropriate, but you can't control the confusing messages on the adult-themed billboard your child is staring at as you drive down the highway.

So, let's begin with differentiating the things you can influence and raising awareness about the things you can't. Both enablers and obstacles lead to valuable opportunities to promote growth and learning.

Name the environmental influences you have some control over. Aspects of your home and its contents might be on your list, along with rules and guidelines for activity and engagement. Whether you decide to home in on a specific problem or expand to your child's entire day, this undertaking will probably spawn some ideas for immediate action. If this is the case, coordinate with family members, if necessary, and begin tackling anything that would benefit from a change.

You'll then be left with the other environmental factors that feel largely out of your hands, or that might take substantial effort to alter—things such as peer influence, birth order, the place where you live, and the pool of available resources in your community. While you can't control these influences, you can factor them into your plans.

As adults, we get to select the community and neighborhood where we raise our children. As children, our parents make that choice for us.

A colleague told me that he grew up in a more diverse environment than his spouse. Hers was decidedly white and upper middle class. His neighborhood was ethnically mixed and financially lower middle class and included the typical experiences that come with such demographics.

They considered raising their children in a community that reflected his norms but elected to establish their family in a place that offered greater economic opportunity and safety—her norms—all at the sacrifice of diversity. As a parent in a similar set of circumstances, I still question the lack of diversity in my kids' environment but appreciate the neighborhood vibe we have chosen. Everything is a trade-off.

Consider the choices you've made and how they influence your child's access to opportunity. Compare that with whatever compromises you may have made in not exposing your child to community hardship. The lack of exposure to hardship may have prevented some coping skills from developing. However, the enhanced exposure to privilege may have created learning and engagement opportunities that otherwise wouldn't have existed.

These are your choices to make. Your kids inherit these decisions. There is no right and wrong—there is simply the shaping of the environment you elect to define your children's life experience. Owning this choice makes parenting a conscious and intentional activity. Awareness of these decisions gives you an edge.

Simply identifying your decisions and recognizing their scope on your child's daily experience will give you a big advantage. Devote some energy to figuring out how each of these influences work as either enablers or obstacles in your child's development. Doing so will help you decide whether it makes sense to increase or decrease their impact.

Let's use technology again as an example, since this is such a big player in many kids' lives these days. What parent isn't concerned about screen time? Whether it's remote learning, social media, or entertainment, our kids are like sponges long before they've developed the coping skills to discern healthy from unhealthy.

For many years, parents were told not to let screens dominate more than two hours of their children's day. Now, screens invade just about every aspect of a child's environment at home, at school, and in the community. How can you have influence?

Much of it is beyond our control. We can't even take our kids to the grocery store or library without some exposure, even if it's just passively watching us use the online card catalog or complete self-check-out. And more significantly, screens pervade endless hours of our children's education, especially as they reach elementary school age. Add a global pandemic and remote-learning realities, and the entire calculus changes.

What if you quit thinking about how to stop the exposure, and instead thought about how to craft the message being sent? You have the gift of being able to set the tone for how your child perceives and engages with the technology that surrounds them. Modeling responsible stewardship goes a long way.

Have conversations about the benefits and pitfalls of all that screens offer, and try to explain your reasoning in developmentally friendly ways. Acknowledge the struggles of their position (maybe their friends "get to play online whenever they want!") with empathy while making sure to hold firm on yours. In the end, your family's circumstances and priorities must rule the day.

> *Your child begins to adopt family culture norms from an earlier age than you might expect, and it's easier for them to do so when the messages are consistent.*

The same goes for peer influence, birth order, and all of the other primarily unchangeable enablers and obstacles in your child's life. Your child's perception of the role they play is a reflection of your modeling. What family culture are you creating?

Set the expectations for how these influences should be perceived and handled, and trust that your child will slowly embrace responsible ownership. Their responses to environmental factors will be based on the guidance you've given and the example you've set. Remember, the dog wags the tail. The tail doesn't wag the dog.

It's a dangerous trap to allow the peer influence of neighborhood, classmate, or extended family opinion to undermine your instincts as parents. Most kids will harness the power of those circles to divide and conquer when they aren't getting their way. Don't forget who is in charge of the family.

> *There are predictable developmental phases when power and control skills are being tested. This is when families are at risk of letting the "tail wag the dog." Kids who are striving for mastery can get too big for their britches. The neighborhood, community culture, and societal vibe are not always supportive when you're trying to hold the line.*

You don't have to answer to societal norms or whatever your kids' friends' parents decide is best. Your family culture is yours to shape. We all cull lessons from our families of origin, close friends, and trusted experts. Once you've gathered the data, engage your critical thinking skills to decide what works best in your family. Sometimes, that'll leave you feeling like a lone voice against a choir of popular sentiment.

The circumstances will obviously vary, but the idea remains the same. During the Covid-19 era, it might have come in the form of a neighbor who offered up playdates but you were concerned about their mask protocols, or that they failed to quarantine after a winter trip to Florida. It's OK to decline something (as awkward as the conversation might be) if your family culture holds to different norms.

The examples are endless. Most are adult versions of the peer pressure we experienced as adolescents, long before we owned accountability for raising children. Whatever the situation, your critical thinking skills will shed light on whether the issue is an enabler or an obstacle. Once that is clear, you will learn the direction that's best for your family's unique circumstances.

If you were asked to design a pre-teen's fantasy hangout, you'd probably make it look something like Izzy and Gio's loft. It was equipped with all of the entertainment and technology a middle-schooler could desire. The siblings' good fortune didn't end there, either.

Both were enrolled in the right activities to give them an edge. Izzy was in her 10th year of dance and her fourth on an elite poms squad. Gio had been involved in premier football and baseball clubs since second grade. They also each had weekly classes at the local academic enrichment center.

Their parents felt secure they couldn't possibly provide for their kids any better. It did make them a little uncomfortable to realize Izzy and Gio would never know what it was like to want things (at least not like they had experienced in their families of origin). They realized long ago that they'd developed a culture of expectation with their kids, if not full-blown entitlement.

Yet it was impossible not to, they reasoned. In their town, everyone started enrichment and sports early. They didn't want their kids to fall behind. And they certainly didn't want them to be socially stunted by the mere fact of not having all the same things as their peers.

Knowing that the kids were scheduled with the right activities and well provided for made their behavior even more perplexing. Izzy could usually be found working on her dance routines or focused on homework. Her parents were proud of the fact she was driven, but unfortunately, she seemed listless and discontented.

Gio, on the other hand, seemed to lack motivation. He flitted from thing to thing with good humor, but never really applied himself. He tended to under perform both in school and in sports. He didn't seem to take anything seriously—other than his dedication to his phone, YouTube, and video games.

Gio inadvertently put a crucial puzzle piece into place for his parents one day. They overheard him talking to friends in the loft: "Whatever...I actually kinda hate football." Just that snippet of a sentence turned their perception upside down. But surely he wanted to do it—it was the highest-profile sport in town! How could he say that? If he felt that way, what else were they getting wrong? It was time for a family meeting.

Gio was up front once the door to conversation was opened. He didn't "really care" about all that stuff. He didn't like practicing things when they took so much time and effort, and there was always something more fun waiting for him anyway. Why work so hard?

Izzy required some coaxing. She knew that she was supposed to "be" all the things her parents envisioned, and wanted to be those things, too. Didn't she? If she wasn't a good student and a talented dancer, who was she?

Izzy and Gio's parents decided it was time for an overhaul. After much discussion, they made a controversial decision to cut the kids' after-school activities to just one each—and they let the kids choose. They reduced pressure by scaling back the intensity as well. No need to specialize in elite classes for now.

Most controversial of all, they established better guidelines for the extra time at home. Gio needed less screen time without all the tech his friends had and more support to improve his engagement and focus. Izzy needed less structured activity and more permission not to achieve and perform.

The positive transformation in their kids wasn't overnight, but the change was undeniable. The increased freedom to figure out what each of them really needed and wanted allowed their unique lights to shine a little brighter. As it turned out, the community's one-size-fits-all model just wasn't a good fit for their children, or their family.

Of course, this decision would run against the grain of neighborhood and community culture expectations. Gio and Izzy's parents weighed this carefully. Widening the lens, they heeded the lessons communicated by their kids' behavior and adjusted the environment accordingly.

MAKING IT STICK

All kinds of enablers and obstacles lurk in every aspect of our children's daily experience. They're found in physical spaces and items, schedule demands, and social messaging, and they're always changing. As kids develop and their worlds expand, parents have less awareness and control of the many influences in their children's activities. The good news is that you can equip your child with the skills to recognize and harness personal enablers and obstacles to their benefit.

Start in your home. This forms the baseline for what kids come to view as normal. How do you design the workstations and play areas? What is the typical noise level, and what happens when one or more family members get distracted? Is the home orderly or cluttered? Are there routines and rhythms that define your household?

> *Every home has a vibe and flow that is unique to the family. Any outsider would detect it as soon as they entered your space. Give thought to the way you want people to move in your space and the vibe your home conveys when the pace of activity ebbs and flows.*

How do mornings begin? How do evenings end? When do things ramp up and why? How do you settle things down when the buzz becomes unproductive?

You get to set the stage for your child every day. This begins with the physical and social environment of your home as you craft the way your child can interact with their immediate surroundings. It then expands to the messages and influences your child is primed to internalize with your continued support.

HOW WILL I KNOW ISSUES HAVE BEEN SUCCESSFULLY ADDRESSED?

Once the messages and influences are internalized, your home becomes a touchstone from which kids can venture out, explore the world, and return for processing and refueling. However you choose to shape the enablers (tools and resources) and obstacles (struggles and limits) in your family, the normalization of rhythms and routines becomes a source of wellness for the kids. They know where to find things and can predict what reaction will follow the actions they take.

They can experiment with new behaviors in an environment that has been made safe by the careful and intentional choices of their caregivers. Enablers get harnessed for growth and obstacles get leveraged for learning. In time, your adjustments get internalized and coping skills grow.

Success is celebrated when you see your child carrying out the messages and strategies you've worked to instill. For young children, it will be seen in the way they directly interact with the people and objects in their surroundings. For older children, it'll be evident in how they navigate their expanding world by seizing their opportunities and taking ownership over their reactions to challenges.

It seems to take forever for maturity to bring new coping skills to the forefront. Watching our kids struggle as these abilities push forward is painful. We just want them to turn the corner. Whether propelled by an enabler or taught a lesson by an obstacle, all kids eventually do manage to get around the corner. Sometimes, it takes a little help from our support systems.

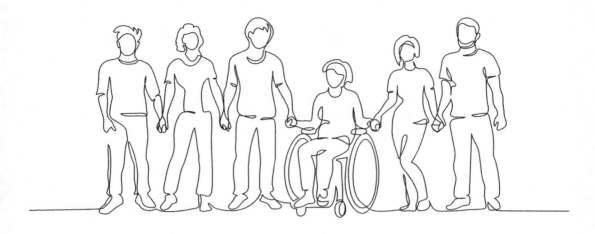

CHAPTER 8

YOUR SUPPORT SYSTEMS

IDENTIFYING THE IMPACT

Now it's time to explore the mainstays of your community that have the power to assist in fulfilling your family's goals. Some larger support systems are non-negotiables in your family's wellness, and they deserve regular check-ups. We'll determine what they are, identify any holes in your network, and start figuring out how to fill them.

You might have great intentions and elaborate plans for your child, but without a foundation of support, you won't end up getting very far. Support systems provide the platforms that make lasting and sustainable improvements possible. Does your family have access to appropriate support for all your needs?

There are some fundamental supports you need while raising a family. Although there will likely be many other unique elements within your ideal toolbox, let's begin by naming the five basic components of a well-functioning, comprehensive support system:

- Access to adequate healthcare
- Readily available childcare
- Sufficient income
- Appropriate education options
- Trusted and reliable counsel

Ideally, these individual support systems link together to form a solid bedrock for your family. In a perfect world, you don't even need to think about them. They just exist in your family's ecosystem and provide everything you need. But there are many degrees of each, and your need to prioritize them will ebb and flow over time.

Think of these five basic components of your support system as proverbial spinning plates. As long as the centrifugal force is keeping them spinning, you have what you need. Occasionally, an environmental demand will cause one of the plates to wobble, requiring you to give it a spin.

Whatever unique, expected, and unexpected changes occur, the point is to keep them all spinning. When one falls, the other four must carry the burden until the disruption is addressed. Think about the many ways that shifts in these five basic components of your support system can change your priorities.

When you have a child with special medical needs, there will be periods when healthcare will rise to the top. If you have pressing work demands, childcare could become your primary concern. In the event of a job loss, everything else might need to take a back seat while you find ways to reestablish income.

Inappropriate educational provisions are likely to upend or negate the rest of the growth supports you have in place for your child.

And if you have nowhere to turn for counsel when you hit a rough patch and don't know how to proceed, any other movement forward can quickly grind to a halt. Having flexibility and dexterity in the system matters.

You'll probably be able to make adjustments to the plates that occasionally go off-kilter. However, the effort of keeping all the plates spinning when one or more is consistently lopsided takes a big toll. This is why the holistic wellness of the system deserves attention. Keeping all elements of your support system in balance matters.

The value of a support system goes beyond its value to a family's functioning. Your resource framework also serves to support family, social, and emotional wellness. When all is right with support systems, you get to enjoy a smooth flow, and the momentum that builds enables positive growth and interaction. Family members and relationships benefit from the freedom that comes with security.

Missing, bruised, or damaged pieces will have the opposite effect. The weight of balancing all components of the family's support system is already a heavy load for caregivers to shoulder. It becomes exponentially heavier whenever any of the components are in disrepair. Any stress that a caregiver experiences as a result of an inadequate support system has a ripple effect on the whole family, including its youngest members.

Think about the subtle yet powerful impact of anything that detracts from a caregiver's ability to be fully engaged. A brief environmental distraction has only a momentary frustration effect on the child yearning for connection or attention, but prolonged emotional trauma creates a more lasting consequence.

Postpartum depression is the most obvious example. When a mom must expend psychic energy maintaining her own wellness, her ability to be fully present for others is compromised. The newborn might receive the bulk of what she has available to give while the older siblings may feel the deficit.

Less obvious examples abound. Look at the anxiety spectrum, for instance. On the mild side of the continuum, a mom's worry can have a contagious impact on a child.

When the parent worries, the child worries.

When stress escalates to generalized anxiety, the caregiver redirects attention to their internal state, thus subtracting from the ability to be attentive to others. More disabling forms of anxiety (obsessive-compulsive disorder, panic attacks, phobias) hijack the caregiver's ability to be engaged in the needs of others.

Prior to the publication of the *Diagnostic and Statistical Manual of Mental Disorders, 5th Edition* (DSM-5), mental health was classified in a five-axis model. The system evaluated mood, personality, medical factors, psycho-social stressors, and level of functioning. Although this system is no longer used by the American Psychiatric Association, the measurement domains are extremely valuable in thinking about the sources of impact on kids.

One, some, or all (mood, personality, medical factors, psycho-social stressors, and level of functioning) are usually in play in most families.

WIDENING THE LENS

When you're ready to assess the gaps that currently exist in your family's support systems, go where your gut takes you. Although some areas won't appear to be blue-ribbon perfect on paper, you may be feeling fairly satisfied when you evaluate the sum and substance of each. This isn't a time to do a "keeping up with the Joneses" exercise— instead, search your heart for the things that genuinely matter to you and that contribute to your family's well-being and functioning.

We're all social creatures. It's nearly impossible not to gauge our standing through comparison with others, or by internalizing others' opinions about what's best for us. Societal pressure has an impact on our perceptions, whether we're talking about the size of our house and how to fill it, the classes and enrichment activities in which we enroll our kids, or the medical interventions we decide to pursue.

Try to identify and give shape to this layer of external influence. Then peel it away to see what lies underneath. What remains are your core values and priorities. The simplicity of this baseline allows you to add only the support and resources that meet the unique needs of your family system. Lay it bare as often as you need to help you stay focused on your priorities.

Few families cover all their complex needs with solely internal re-sources. This is where the trusted counsel part of your support system comes into play. Because we're social creatures, we all crave the opportunity to learn from others. Engaging in conversation helps us explore and develop our thoughts, feelings, and ideas differently than thinking on our own. The need for collaboration is rarely more poignant than when it comes to parenting.

Stressors can make us feel like we're lost in the weeds of our thoughts and experiences. They bog us down and stall decision-making. Because it is natural to withdraw and close ranks when under stress, we are likely to cut off the resources we need most when our families are under duress. But it shouldn't take a crisis to solicit help.

Close friends, family members, and your vetted professional team

*members hold the key to helping you clear a path forward. Allow
a trusted person to hold up a mirror for you to see things more
clearly.*

Your sources of support are at your disposal. Ask them to assist
in highlighting the elements that should have more of your attention.
If you're still feeling stuck, enlist as many partners as you need to encourage you to shift your perspective, help you identify the barriers to
accessing the right support systems, and set you up for action.

TAKING ACTION

After you've gained some clarity about your family's specific needs and
how well your support systems are measuring up, you can begin to fill
in the cracks. Some bigger holes will require more time for repair. The
goal is simply to begin taking steps, one at a time.

If the task at hand feels overwhelming, break it down. Pick one
actionable item—no matter how tiny—to help gain some traction.
Information gathering is a good place to start. For example, if your
child's educational options aren't up to par based on their needs, put
some feelers out to peers who might be experiencing a similar problem.
Have they discovered solutions that might also work for your family?

There might be good alternatives that exist just outside of your
awareness. Send an email to the teachers and education professionals
in your circle. Express your concerns and ask for ideas. Search for sup-
plemental resources you can employ at home or in your community.
Once you've gathered some ideas, cull the list and spend some additional time learning more about each option.

You can make improvements in any of the areas (healthcare,
childcare, income, education, and trusted counsel) as needed by fol-

lowing this simple cycle: Research, plan, execute, assess, repeat. The process applies whether you need alternative healthcare options, an improved financial situation, more childcare, better suited education options, or additional support relationships. Make sure you stick to it until you feel comfortable with each part of your system.

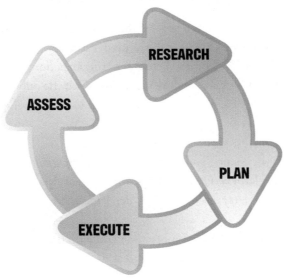

The *research-plan-execute-assess-repeat* cycle is based on a continuous improvement process. Your environment is always changing, as are the skills and capacities of your kids. The family and larger support network are in a constant state of adjusting to these changes. A continuous improvement approach allows you to shape and steer the change with some strategy.

> *Study the big picture. Craft an adaptation. Try it out. Evaluate how it worked. Do it again (and again and again and again). Each stage of the continuous improvement process has unique challenges that make keeping the cycle moving difficult.*

It's important not to get bogged down in planning. If it helps, give yourself an artificial deadline to take the first step on just one item. When faced with challenges, any movement forward is the best path to feeling better. Things may not change as quickly as you would like, but every time you alter the landscape, you create footholds to propel yourself in the right direction.

This is the assess function of the continuous improvement cycle. Not every plan works once it is executed. Of course, you weighed the pros and cons of each option before selecting an action, but sometimes you have to go back to the drawing board. Keep the outcome in mind (adapting to the change in the environment to strengthen your stable of support systems).

*There are many paths to the same destination, so the **research-plan-execute-assess-repeat** process allows you to experiment and retry when something doesn't work as expected.*

Some changes require more time and patience than others. Lasting success is often the result of a great deal of trial and error, but it's worth the struggle. Setbacks are normal.

Sometimes things get worse before they get better.

It's an ongoing task to build better support systems for yourself and your family. Give yourself some grace whenever it feels insurmountable. Keeping your eye on the prize will give you fuel.

I t had been tough for Jen to find suitable learning experiences for Grace throughout her first few years. Now Grace had just turned 6 and Jen had a new but hopefully much easier mission: simply usher her into the local elementary school program. Piece of cake, right?

Grace had a special spark. She was imaginative and fun-loving. She was determined and strong. And as it turned out, she didn't fit any mold that her school district had in place.

It had been clear early on that Grace experienced the world through a unique lens and learned differently than her peers. She received therapy sessions through their local early intervention system as a toddler, followed by a preschool program that had extra therapy support built in. Although it wasn't always smooth sailing, Grace enjoyed the experiences and had blossomed.

Then kindergarten began. Her new educational team recommended that Grace begin in a smaller classroom with more adult support. Jen worried that it would be an overly restrictive environment with less academic rigor and a less motivating peer dynamic, but she agreed to the plan. They were the experts, after all.

Unfortunately, it didn't take long to figure out something was off. Although things appeared to start out OK and her teachers and therapists were optimistic, Grace was faltering. She protested getting on the bus each morning, tried to bolt out of her classroom at every opportunity, and had begun to display some concerning new aggressive behaviors both at school and at home.

Jen's gut told her that Grace was reacting to being in an environment that frustrated her. She had entered school with an age-appropriate reading level, which was already beginning to decline. Her math scores were also surprisingly low when compared with what Jen saw at home. Most significantly, she was losing her spark.

Several months and several team meetings later, Jen felt

like they were at an impasse with what the school was able to offer. She had been receiving support and information from a couple of friends who had found a suitable alternative program for their own kids in the next town over, which housed a larger school district with more options. Based on everything she'd learned, she knew in her heart it was what Grace needed. Maybe it was time to make the change.

But there was a huge hurdle—they would need to move in order to qualify for enrollment. This was overwhelming. Jen relied heavily on her friends for encouragement and reassurance as she let the idea settle in. She then spent what felt like an eternity going over options with her husband. They toured the new school together, plus two others. In the end, they decided it was the right decision for Grace's future and their family's wellness.

Once the decision was made, momentum took over. There were brief moments of panic and self-doubt and tension, but overall, Jen was bolstered by the knowledge that there was hope on the horizon. "No pain, no gain" became her motto. Fortunately, all the difficulty paid off.

After a transition period, Grace acclimated surprisingly well. She made friends, stopped protesting school, and accelerated her learning pace—and her aggressive behaviors declined. Her spark was reignited, and it made the upheaval worthwhile. When the dust eventually settled, Jen also discovered an unexpected bonus: the positive change in her own spirit and energy was undeniable.

MAKING IT STICK

Just as with the other areas we've explored, the shape, fit and strength of your support systems will shift over time. The quality of support available to you will change continuously, as will your family's specific requirements. Low priorities become high priorities without warning, and apparent emergencies sometimes solve themselves.

> *Your job is to keep an eye on how well the available resources remain matched up to your needs over each phase of your child's development.*

Some gaps that appear in your support systems will be acutely felt. A job loss, medical emergency, education crisis, or sudden void in childcare will result in a triage situation that necessitates immediate action. While difficult and stressful to address, these types of events won't require special attention to make themselves apparent.

But a trickier scenario exists. Some gaps will form more insidiously and probably won't be as readily noticeable. They'll begin as hairline cracks formed by resource inadequacy, rather than absence, and become normalized as you adapt to them—even as they continue to grow dangerously under your feet.

Those hairline cracks are no laughing matter. They present a significant risk precisely because of their subtlety. By making it a habit to regularly assess if your evolving needs are being met in the way you'd like, you're able to shine a light on danger zones early enough so that they, too, don't become triage situations.

HOW WILL I KNOW ISSUES HAVE BEEN SUCCESSFULLY ADDRESSED?

Spend a few minutes every so often evaluating your resource fitness. Look at each component and consider whether your family might benefit from changes to any of the five essential pillars of support: *healthcare, childcare, income, education, counsel.* When a gap is identified, no matter how small, it's time to re-employ the research-plan-execute-assess-repeat cycle.

You won't be able to wave a magic wand and make everything fall into place during each phase of your family and child's developmental course. But regular assessment of each pillar's strength is the surest way to keep them standing upright over the long haul.

And remember, most of the lessons learned with Child #1 will not work with Child #2 (and, in turn, #3). Because each child's personality is different, the support network might be different, too.

CHAPTER 9

YOUR CHILD'S READINESS

IDENTIFYING THE IMPACT

All parents are aware that no two kids are alike. Every baby is born already possessing a unique set of traits. You might even be able to detect some of them from the womb, as I found out. My most physically driven son's in-utero gymnastics woke me out of sound sleep regularly before he even took his first breath, while my quietest son had me doing doctor-prescribed kick-counts throughout my pregnancy just to make sure he was still OK in there.

Neuropsychologists paint a picture of foundation elements forming very early in the life span. In fact, in the brief window of time from 42 days post-conception to three years post-birth, all of the neurological connections needed for any strength or talent are established (100 billion neurons!). From about age 3 to age 16, about 50% of these neurological axons, dendrites, and synaptic connections shed away, leaving the uniqueness of each child to form in partnership with countless environmental variables.

Each child's inborn traits—things like activity level, curiosity, perseverance, self-awareness, confidence, playfulness, and desire for engagement—interact to form what we commonly call disposition. Your child's unique traits also intermingle with environmental messages over time to develop their capacity for trust, an awareness of their emerging knowledge base, and an attitude toward learning.

You'll probably notice similarities between siblings or recognize links between your own habits and preferences and your child's. We've all enjoyed the game of trying to determine which elements of a child's personality come from which family members. The truth is that all outward behavior results from a mix of both nature and nurture.

We're products of our environment. Identical twins sharing DNA are often born with different dispositions due to varying experiences in utero, and the difference only expands with age. Minute by minute, the outside world either vindicates or refutes the value of our reactions to it. We then make tiny adjustments. These feedback loops are endless. After a while, our little adjustments add up to big shifts in our perspectives and the way we move through the world.

Think about a time when you felt competent and successful. What was it about the people, activity, or setting that brought out the best in you? How well did everything jive with your natural inclinations?

Now juxtapose that with a time you're not proud of how you handled something. What was different? I'm willing to bet that the situation demanded that you step out of your comfort zone and draw upon some traits you don't naturally possess. These are simple examples of those natural proclivities that begin forming in the first three years of life and get shaped with each experience thereafter.

If a specific time of day or activity continues to give you (and your child) difficulty, look beyond the factors we've discussed in prior chapters. Look past the expectations, interpersonal dynamics, developmental fit, enablers and obstacles, and support systems to determine if a disposition misfit might also be part of the problem. When something isn't working, your child's behavioral response will be your first clue to a mismatch between readiness and expectations.

Whenever a mismatch occurs, a child is set up to fail. Natural strengths and weaknesses make them either well prepared or leave them underprepared to manage challenges, which means all the difference in being able to face situations effectively.

Later in the life span, we're all able to strengthen areas of weakness. But expecting a child to perform well with an unnatural skillset is unfair. When you factor in natural strengths and weaknesses, you become much more patient when your child is struggling. There's usually a reason for both fast and slow adaptation.

It might seem like an unnecessary step, but consider writing down your child's traits. Or even better, describe them aloud to someone else. Ideally, share them with someone who also knows your child intimately and can make valuable additions to the conversation.

You'll be surprised by how much the exercise helps you see the powerful connection between your child's innate way of moving through life and their behavioral responses. And in a larger way, it'll highlight the influence their personality has on their growth and learning. Determining what comes from nature and what comes from nurture can be tricky.

WIDENING THE LENS

Identifying the personality traits that your child brings to the table is only half the battle (admittedly an important half). One of my graduate school professors used to preach the importance of the balance between nature and nurture. When I shared a side conversation with him later in both of our careers, he conceded that he no longer saw it as 50/50. Nature, he suggested, frequently wins the coin flip when trying to figure out why we are who we are.

While still acknowledging the essential role of nurture, this chapter is about paying attention to our kids' inborn baselines. The University of Chicago began researching the interplay among motivation, capacity, and opportunity over a half-century ago. In researcher Lilian Ripple's *Social Service Monographs, Second Series*, she referenced a "built-in capacity for change." Ripple postulated that the interplay among motivation, capacity, and opportunity were key to problem-solving.

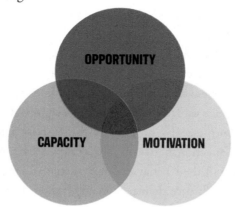

So, your next task is to determine whether your child is displaying the necessary motivation and capacity to take advantage of available opportunities. Are personality traits being triggered by a situation helpful? Providing open-ended free time may call out one child's creativity, while it might cause another to feel depleted and listless.

The exact reverse might be true for a structured activity offered to the same pair of kids. The best circumstances will be tailor-fit with the unique personality strengths of your child. It's a sure bet that environmental feedback will draw out some traits more than others. This is the beauty of the nature/nurture balance—each influence activates the other.

If you want to know how your kid is wired, keep an eye on which abilities soar when they are faced with a challenge. Personality shapes the environment, and the environment shapes personality.

Devote some attention to identifying which traits are typically expressed by your child in moments of difficulty and which ones are on display when they're able to shine (surprisingly, they might be the same). Then try to apply that knowledge to what you see throughout the day. Use their reactions to situations as a sign of readiness for whatever it is you'd like them to do.

"Readiness" isn't just an indication of developmental stage. More often, it's a signal about whether the challenge is matching up with natural disposition. When it does, the child seems to move with ease. When it doesn't, the struggle is giving you an important message to consider.

Your child is always ready for growth under the right conditions. Situations need to spark engagement if they're going to be successful. This is similar to figuring out if developmental levels are part of why something is or isn't working, but there's a crucial difference. In this exercise, you're focusing on emotional response to the situation. Curiosity, capacity for trust, and a positive attitude toward learning are best elevated whenever an activity fits with a child's preferences.

Potty training and learning to read are a couple of classic examples for many children. Developmental readiness is always modified by peer influence. As parents learn quickly, the harder you push the more resistance you get. Yet, things seem to fall into place when the neighbor kids or classmates are all doing it.

Consider the interactions your child experiences in both your home and community. Are there any missed opportunities? There are bound to be times when your child isn't ready for what a situation is offering. However, there'll be just as many examples of times when your child is poised for learning, yet the external conditions aren't set up to match their readiness.

Kids will often show subtle signs that they are ready to take things up a notch, whether by learning a new skill, assuming more responsibility, increasing independence, or expanding social connections. These moments call upon your parenting skills as a diagnostician. See if you can decipher the "why."

Whether a child is on target with developmental milestones is rarely driven simply by age. The "windows" of development don't open and shut in one fell swoop. Sometimes we might catch a glimmer of initiative or an expression of pride when something new works, only to be met with resistance the next time we encourage our child to repeat the task.

The span of acquisition is wide and influenced by innumerable factors. But we can always help our kids grow at their ideal rate by paying attention to their cues for interest. A child's disposition is a reliable indicator of their readiness for growth and learning. When opportunities arise, natural strengths are empowered and natural weaknesses are challenged.

Meaningful engagement does wonders for creating a lasting skill. There's a long list of research illustrating the benefit of volition on the acquisition of new skills. Brain pathways for new experiences are laid and reinforced best when a child is fully invested in their own learning. On the other hand, imposing learning experiences on your child without their buy-in will only serve to frustrate both parties.

Rather than becoming discouraged by your child's resistance, try to respect their pace and provide low-pressure opportunities for them to try new experiences on for size. Wait until they're ready, and honor resistance as a clue. Children often use behavior rather than words to communicate their preparedness for growth.

As caregivers, our job is to pay attention to these signals and finesse the child's exposure to challenges accordingly. Kids have a way of telling us whether they need time to strengthen their foundation or that they are ready to be pushed. Both mastery and struggle have messages that drive the effectiveness of our parenting approach— we need to listen to the language of behavior.

TAKING ACTION

You have the power to harness your child's engagement by understanding and leveraging their unique personality traits and readiness. Let's think about the practical application in day-to-day terms. Each unfolding moment provides a signal that offers a red/yellow/green clue.

Start with your daily homelife. It's usually easiest to begin with the difficult situations or things that clearly aren't working while at home. There are probably predictable times when your child shuts down or tunes you out, doesn't follow directions, or acts out. Think about these specific situations and try to identify which parts of the task are likely butting up against your child's readiness to participate.

Maybe your child is easily overwhelmed by a lot of environmental stimuli, and the situation is filled with people, noise, and visual distractions. Perhaps your child craves a lot of touch and movement, and the situation is preventing that need fulfillment. If your child is the type who likes seeing something all the way through, abrupt transitions will probably throw them off.

Or it could be that your child is a "non-linear thinker" and feels stifled or confused by having to follow concrete instructions that don't resonate with their natural thought processes. Some disposition clues are obvious while others are subtle. Parents are usually the experts when it comes to deciphering the code.

Use the list of personality traits you've made and highlight the likely speed bumps (or the "yellow" in our traffic signal). Keeping that knowledge in your back pocket will help you exercise patience when things aren't playing out as planned. Likewise, the conclusions about your kid's strengths will be validated whenever you watch them fully engage with innate energy ("green" in our traffic signal).

Now that you've gathered some ideas about what's going wrong with the tough stuff in the day, flip your focus to the moments when everything seems to come together, and think to yourself, "Wow, my kid is really something!"

Knowing the way they like to move through the world, try to identify how the circumstances came together to bring out the very best in your child. Are there ways to apply those things to the problem areas? Find opportunities to experiment with small changes and make adjustments as you learn from them.

At the same time you're making changes at home, you can start thinking about how to bring your understanding to the wider community. Teachers, other caregivers, and healthcare personnel won't always recognize when they're missing clues to readiness or resistance. You know the secret code of your child's communication. Help your support systems understand this language.

> *You know your child better than anyone. You may have to function as an interpreter of your child's signals sometimes.*

The larger the system (schools, community agencies, etc.), the greater the likelihood that the child will be categorized with a generalization, good or bad. Whenever a system generalizes or narrows the perspective on the complex world of a child to a simple label, the understanding of their unique features has been sacrificed for a convenient handle. The caregiver's job is to elevate the subtle nuances that make the child unique to the larger system.

Logan was the first: first child born to Kat (a teacher) and Tom (an athletic trainer), first grandchild, and the first boy in either family in a long while. From the moment his gender was announced, the excited adults indulged themselves in purchasing all the sports/fire truck/dino-themed items they could lay their hands on. The same themes played out on his first birthday, and the basement was soon filled with tiny plastic basketball hoops, climbing equipment, pint-sized vehicles, and balls.

Tom fantasized about the day he'd be able to teach Logan to play catch and couldn't wait to sign him up for his first tot sports classes. As soon as Logan was fully walking, they found an open gym class meant for toddlers. Logan just stood there and watched the kids play. Tom tried to be patient, but his eagerness spilled out via intense encouragement for Logan to run around and try out the equipment. Several sessions ended in tears for Logan and frustration for both.

Similar themes played out throughout Logan's early childhood. They tried Tiny Tots Multi-Sports, basketball, and soccer. They brought Logan to indoor jungle gyms and trampoline parks. Logan enjoyed some sports-themed play at home with playful encouragement. But somehow none of the classes or field trips resonated. In fact, the older he got, the more tightly wound he became in those circumstances.

Although the "sports problem" wasn't a daily occurrence and easy to dismiss, the angst it caused seeped into the whole family dynamic. Tom lost his temper with Logan at times. Why couldn't he just be a "normal" boy? He felt both the frustration of not being able to share his passion with his son and the heat of all the other parents watching as his son cried on the sidelines time and again.

Kat and Tom were at odds about it. Following the first open gym debacle, Kat felt they shouldn't keep pushing Logan out of his comfort zone. Tom felt that it was a critical part of development and he shouldn't be coddled. And Logan's anxiety continued to grow.

By the time T-ball rolled around, Logan was old enough to push back with more than just tears and tantrums. He didn't like it when there were too many people, he told his parents. The other kids were too fast and pushed him.

He was scared of being hit by the ball. He couldn't remember what to do and hated being yelled at. Tom's impulse was to dismiss Logan's protests and tell him to "buck up." But he held back and asked Logan if he'd like a break. Logan's quick answer was yes.

At Kat's suggestion, they used the time for father-son back-yard sports. Logan was an entirely different kid out there. He was happy, giggly, and energetic. His interest and stamina still weren't stellar, but his skills were building along with his confidence. Seeing this made Tom relax and appreciate his son's strengths.

Second grade came and Logan's best friend asked if he was going to play baseball with him. This time the decision was Logan's, and surprisingly, he asked his parents to sign up. Now that the pressure was off and he had some control over his experience, Logan was ready.

He wasn't going to be a "lifer" with organized youth sports, and he would always prefer sitting at home with books and Legos. But Kat and Tom had an important realization: Logan wasn't developing into the timid, easily intimidated kid they had predicted while watching him fall apart during those early experiences. In fact, he was impressively spirited and had a leadership streak. He was simply inclined for less physical pursuits, but he was open to trying things on his own timeline as his confidence grew. They only needed to give him room to find his way and follow his lead.

MAKING IT STICK

Remember that even (especially!) when we think we have our kids pegged, they change. Your shy toddler might turn into the ringleader of their peer group in preschool. Your boisterous preschooler might become an introspective grade-schooler. Most aspects of your child's personality will be a lifelong part of their fabric, but different threads are highlighted within each stage.

Don't take your understanding for granted. Think of that list of traits you prepared as a living and breathing document and be ready to edit it regularly. I was stunned when my extremely reserved, quiet, and emotionally reactive 2-year-old found his voice in the neighborhood peer group. Practically overnight, he transformed into an outgoing comedian.

> *There are always things brewing inside your child that will surprise you. We can't predict the future, and we never want to pigeonhole our kids based only on what we see today.*

A willingness to stay flexible will help you see with greater clarity when shifts are occurring. Your understanding of your child is meant to grow right along with them as they traverse the stages of childhood. The social, physical, and emotional environment is constantly influencing our kids and triggering things in them. The child you see in front of you today might not be the child you greet tomorrow.

Yet it's precisely this constant change and influence of the environment on our kids that makes knowing their wiring important. Until they're in a stage when they can assume full ownership of their strengths and challenges, our kids need help to build upon their assets, leverage their vulnerabilities, and gain confidence. We can do this by regularly responding to their evolving signals of readiness and by helping others within their circle learn to do the same.

The counseling profession refers to the process as "leading." In psychotherapy circles, leading is the clinician's responsibility to predict the client's readiness for insight or a therapeutic nudge. If the therapist pushes too hard or too quickly, the client will resist, shut down, or even regress. Yet when the counselor measures the client's readiness accurately, they "lead" them to insight and growth.

Clinicians use the red/yellow/green principle, too. This analogy helps us see our roles as caregivers similarly. We have stewardship over a constant assessment of our kids' readiness for understanding, learning, and growth. Knowing when to stop, wait, or go is the key.

HOW WILL I KNOW ISSUES HAVE BEEN SUCCESSFULLY ADDRESSED?

It's important to remember that this chapter focuses on adapting the environmental demands surrounding your child to match their wiring, not the other way around. Your child already possesses a unique foundation and timetable of readiness for most things. We don't want to change who they are or how they move through the world (and frankly, any attempt to do so would be frustrating).

The goal is to discover creative ways to tap your child's full potential while honoring their observable stop-and-go lights during each interaction.

In many cases, you'll find ways to make modifications so a situation works with, instead of against, your child's natural inclinations. But other times it simply will make more sense to hit pause. In these cases, success may mean making the decision to stop or pull back on a routine altogether.

This is such a tough call when the activity or routine seems valuable of its own accord. It'll require honest evaluation on your part to determine the reasons for the routine in the first place. Again, widen the lens.

What am I talking about here? Consider all the enrichment activities that promise to give our kids a leg up in their development. The park district classes, music lessons, sports teams or clinics, tutoring, clubs, community events, library programs—plus whatever else may be popular where you live. Sometimes we as parents get caught up in making sure our kids stay caught up.

Our intentions are undoubtedly good, but there's a danger of losing sight of the cost on our child. Having an overly full schedule, even one filled with great activities, will take a cumulative toll. And—here comes a big statement from this pediatric occupational therapist—that may also be true with some of the clinical interventions your child has been receiving.

Are you shepherding or engineering? Over-programming can take many forms—too many extracurricular activities or too much enrichment or too many therapy sessions. Shepherding means we function as guardrails in our decisions about how best to support our kids. This includes everything from the amount of exposure to stimulation to the ebb and flow of their daily schedules.

Sometimes, less is more.

Thinning out your child's routine to just the essentials is hard but can be a worthwhile undertaking. Downtime for reflection, synthesis of information, and free time without parameters is so important in a child's life. Just as sleep (and the dreaming it brings) helps our brains flush out the clutter and restore and prepare for another day, unstructured time gives our kids the space they need to integrate what they've learned and organize their understanding of the world.

Consider the metaphor of a tree's changes from season to season. There is a purpose for the winter's dormancy. The lifeblood of the tree returns to the roots so the energy can be refueled for new growth in the spring. Sometimes, our kids' readiness signals are communicating the need for a reboot.

What season is your child experiencing?

You'll know you've done a good job matching your child's readiness signals to the events and expectations of their day when your child appears able to move through their routines in a smooth and engaged manner. Each season has a specific purpose. You can push forward or pull back. Constant growth is not the objective. Knowing when to push and when not to is the goal.

CHAPTER 10

BRINGING IT ALL TOGETHER

WIDENING THE LENS

If you've made it this far, you have a pretty good idea of all of the many environmental elements that impact your child's learning, behavior, and development. You probably also have some plans in mind to close any gaps you've identified and to keep on promoting the stuff that's working. I encourage you to continually move forward with little changes. When you start to feel overwhelmed, use baby steps to keep things going—once you've begun to see positive changes in your child, the hope is that your momentum will become self-sustaining.

> *Change is often hard to sustain. Family systems tend to follow the rule of "homeostasis," as living organisms seek sameness. In other words, our efforts to make change are in competition with*

the system's desire to regress back to "normal," even if "normal" isn't healthy.

This is why momentum is so important. Once your family creates a new habit, homeostasis protects this new set point. Research varies on how long it takes to make your momentum into a habit. Some say 21 days while others say 30. Either way, the goal is to sustain your change long enough for it to become a norm.

The environmental landscape is always transforming, so reassessment is constant (that's why we have 22 tear-out worksheets in the F.E.A.T. booklet). The domains of the tool don't always grow from "delayed" to "advanced," and that's OK. Each environmental influence ebbs and flows with the family's circumstances. The important thing is to switch your lens regularly enough so you can see the environmental influences for what they are. It's a simple trick to help your kid, but it needs practice to become a habit.

Strengthening your foundation helps your child make more effective connections. These connections empower growth, which, over time, increases resilience. More-resilient kids have stronger foundations to support further cycles of connection and growth.

The cycles continue from childhood to adolescence and well into adulthood. The patterns and themes that characterize our coping skills as grown-ups were established early in life. The foundation provides the platform. The greatest opportunities for strengthening happen during childhood and adolescence, before things get locked in.

NO MISTAKES, JUST OPPORTUNITIES

This is not to say that we can't make changes at any point, both for ourselves and for our kids. It's never too late to establish new patterns and systems when you discover something isn't working as well as you'd like. It just takes a little more discipline as we get older.

My hope is that reading this book has allowed you to slow down and contemplate new ways of understanding your family's and child's circumstances, in ways big and small. It seems like a basic thing, but in the harried pace of life, we don't often take the time to simply look around and gather our thoughts. We'd all do ourselves a favor by sitting back for a beat to consider if the routines we take for granted are leading to the outcomes we want.

Move theory to practice. Certain sections of this book have resonated with you more than others. Page back and take note of the themes you've highlighted, bookmarked, or dog-eared. These are the best places to start. This book is designed to reflect on your family's personal journey. If something caught your attention, it's worthy of action. Start small.

> There isn't a single recipe. The adaptations you select are as unique as your family's themes and the challenges of your family's moment in time.

The idea is to stay alert to themes and challenges. Distill them down to the basics. Maybe wellness anchors everything. Maybe a healthy marriage creates a platform for collaborative parenting. For some families, it's all about balancing and rebalancing priorities. Whatever your family's circumstances demand, design a "treatment plan" to match.

CHANGE DOESN'T HAPPEN IN ISOLATION

Know that any change you make is bound to have a ripple effect on the others. This is expected and absolutely OK. Adjustments made to better meet caregiver needs may impact your child's caregiver situation, and they'll likely need time to adapt. When your child enters a new developmental stage, their readiness for growth and learning will take on new forms as well. New clinical relationships have the potential to alter family routines and schedules in temporary yet uncomfortable ways. The list goes on.

Plans should be created with the potential results of all areas in mind, even while focusing on individual actions within each. Doing so will ensure you're not caught off guard while the inevitable shifts occur.

It's a balancing act, to be sure, but it's not as complicated as you might expect. As long as you're focused on trying new things to facilitate a positive outcome, the odds are good you won't go wrong. And don't forget: there's always an opportunity to try again with something else.

The F.E.A.T. circle was introduced in Chapter 1 as a visual for this.

CHAPTER 10: BRINGING IT ALL TOGETHER

Change is constant for everyone. The goal isn't to have everything perfect in all domains simultaneously. That simply isn't realistic. The shape of each domain in the circle is continually evolving. Imagine the circle—and your family unit—as a living and breathing organism. With every inhalation and exhalation, individual parts shrink and grow. Movement, even when it's happening in smaller ways, is perpetual.

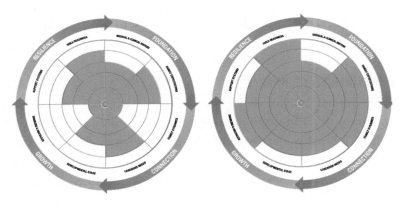

SEIZING LITTLE OPPORTUNITIES IN REAL TIME

One of the biggest enemies of action is overindulgence in big-scale thinking. Stop and take a deep breath if you catch yourself projecting too far into the future ("What will this problem mean for him as a high schooler in 10 years?" or, "I know she's only 3 now, but she'll never make it in kindergarten if we don't figure this out!"). It's also important to stop yourself from trying to overhaul everything at once.

Remind yourself to bring your focus down—way down. Tuck whatever ideas you've gathered while reading the earlier chapters under your arm so they're at the ready, and apply them a little bit at a time whenever it feels right. This book is meant to be bookmarked for future reference.

Not everything applies right now. But you'll be ready when you return to the bookmark. Be decisive and try things as they occur to you. The worst that can happen is that they don't work and you'll reverse course or try something different next time.

Stay on the lookout for naturally occurring opportunities to make minor alterations. I guarantee you'll find a comfortable place to start, whether you're working on your physical space, interpersonal relationships, new intervention strategies, or the creation of better support systems. Small changes will eventually add up to some big differences.

REMEMBERING YOUR "WHY"

There will be plenty of chances to do the research; make the phone calls; write the emails; and rearrange your spaces, tools, and processes little by little. If you find yourself devoting energy to those things at the expense of regular time and connection with your child, it might be time to take a breather. At the heart of all your intentions, planning, and hard work is a kiddo waiting in the wings for your direct attention and affection.

Part of the recipe is simply reminding yourself to see what's in front of you. Right now—at this very moment!—you have an amazing and beautifully complex marvel of nature in your care.

You and your child deserve at least some small part of the day when you can cast all of the thinking and planning aside, and do nothing else but appreciate and enjoy one another. Varying schedules and life demands require some flexibility, but fitting in even five minutes now and then will have a surprising impact. What's your favorite way to do this?

My favorite opportunities occur at meals and bedtime. I like to spend a few minutes sitting back and soaking in each of my kids during dinner—their moods, how they're changing, what's important to them that particular day. (Lest you imagine a picture-perfect scene, please allow me to reassure you—it always crumbles soon after when our usual chaos takes over, with siblings provoking each other, people leaving their seats for various reasons, and the dog distracting us with attempts to score food.)

I then try to carve out several more minutes during nightly tuck-ins for more intimate one-on-one conversations and the simple pleasure of being together. It doesn't work out beautifully every evening, and I often have to squeeze it in quicker than I'd like. But there's never been a time when I haven't found it to be 100% worth the effort.

GROWTH IS CYCLICAL

The beauty of development is that kids get many chances. If something goes well, it is delivered to the stages of growth that follow. If there is a struggle, a future stage will provide a new opportunity to master the skill. Each stage of the cycle has a specific purpose that feeds the needs of the next stage.

Throughout childhood and adolescence, life challenges repeat. Each repetition provides kids an opportunity to solidify gains and create new pathways for development. Erik Erikson's theory (see Chapter 6) provides a sophisticated understanding of each stage. But let's simplify the conversation as we pull everything together in this chapter.

The foundation of human development begins with attachment. Kids enter the world with a set of tools that enable them to connect—first with their primary caregivers and then with others. This is when basic trust is established. This connection allows them to explore and learn from their environment.

At that point, external limits start becoming internalized. The resulting self-control promotes a phase of growth defined by mastery of social-emotional coping skills. This mastery forms a platform for independence that, by its nature, allows the child to seek the next level of connection though trust-enabled attachment.

As the cycle progresses, each skill is strengthened. At any given moment, there is more than one developmental phase in play. As self-control and autonomy are taking shape, a new stage of attachment and exploration is already unfolding. The Epigenetic Principle illustrates this cyclical process.

The Epigenetic Principle
(Erik Erikson)
*Every developmental stage
inherits both the successes and
failures of the previous stages.*

Our kids get many chances

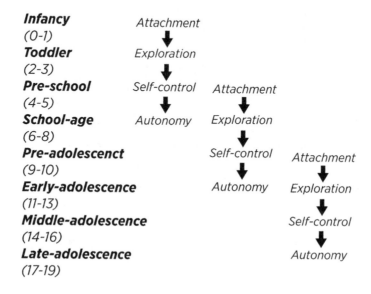

Infancy (0-1) — Attachment
Toddler (2-3) — Exploration
Pre-school (4-5) — Self-control — Attachment
School-age (6-8) — Autonomy — Exploration
Pre-adolescenct (9-10) — Self-control — Attachment
Early-adolescence (11-13) — Autonomy — Exploration
Middle-adolescence (14-16) — Self-control
Late-adolescence (17-19) — Autonomy

Think about where your child is operating within the cycle. Where they are today will give you a clue to the next stage they're entering, even if it's currently invisible.

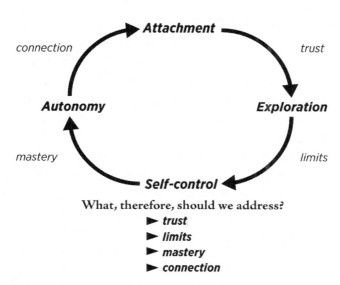

What, therefore, should we address?
▶ *trust*
▶ *limits*
▶ *mastery*
▶ *connection*

As you can see in the graphic, the cycles overlap. The completion of one shares functions with the beginning of the next. Rather than looking at your child's age, think about their current challenges in the context of past and future development. You can better understand their struggles when you're considering environmental disruptions that either recently impacted their mastery, are currently exerting an influence, or are predictably around the corner.

Now try to flip your lens using that knowledge. Instead of considering your child's developmental challenges, look at where they are trying to grow. For example, if they are behaving in a clingy way, maybe they're working on trust. If they've been defiant, perhaps they are exploring their environment and trying to internalize external limits.

You get it. Self-control and increased autonomy follow. These phases might be times when they're acting too big for their britches. As your child is fine-tuning these stages, they're setting the stage for the next ones. The examples are infinite, but the cycles are predictable.

PARTNERING WITH THE COMMUNITY

You're never alone in your parenting journey. A sizable cast of characters is already part of your child's world, from the time they are born. No matter the particulars of your family's circle, many people share in shaping your child's learning and growth. These people can be an indispensable source of support for both you and your child whenever challenges arise.

We're all prone to having subconscious role expectations for ourselves and others. It's easy to take those internalized roles for granted. Patterns become established and slowly transform over time without much conscious consideration. Homeostasis then takes over.

The result is that some important voices can become undervalued while other, perhaps less-deserving voices take over. Even if those bigger voices are helpful in their way, they may be overshadowing someone who also has something useful to offer. Consider if this might be true in your family.

Do you have any opportunities to elevate the influence of some immediate or extended family members whose support would be appropriate given your current circumstances?

Ask yourself the same question regarding your circle of friends, your neighbors, and your network of expert professionals. Who might be waiting in the wings to contribute a solution or helping hand? Many of us feel hesitant to ask "outsiders" for help, imagining we'll be imposing on people, taking advantage of their good nature, or exposing our shortcomings.

The truth is that by asking a trusted person for help, we're strengthening a mutual collaboration that's probably just as gratifying for them. I get a great deal of satisfaction from knowing that I may have lightened a fellow parent's load or made their experience smoother, and every exchange contributes to my own growth as well. This holds true whether I'm functioning as a neighbor, friend, or professional.

When my first son was born, I was convinced that I should be able to do everything myself. I felt a self-imposed pressure to handle whatever came my way. Without realizing it, I built up an emotional barrier to accepting assistance, much less letting myself ask for it. As a young parent, I wanted to appear competent.

Following far too many anxious days and sleepless nights with a colicky infant, I tearfully bundled him up into his stroller for a sunrise walk one summer morning to clear my head. I had the good fortune of running into a neighbor (and seasoned mother) who immediately assessed the situation and offered comfort, camaraderie, and invaluable advice. While I never would have sought her counsel on my own, that short conversation on the sidewalk ended up making a huge difference for me during a difficult period.

On a different occasion, I was at a local park having a conversation with another mom while our kids scaled the playground equipment. It had been a particularly challenging couple of weeks with my youngest child. Without prompting, the mom offered an observation that reawakened a discovery I had made nearly a decade prior. "Have you ever noticed…," she thought out loud, "…how sometimes a growth spurt happens right after your kid drives you to the brink of losing your mind?"

I sat in silence as I recalled stumbling upon the same insight early in my parenting journey. Back then, the breakthrough was language and the newfound ability to express something my son wasn't previously able to communicate. On the playground, I witnessed a new physical ability that enabled him to navigate his world more easily. Increased strength and balance led him to test out some of the "big boy" equipment on the playground.

He showed confidence in places that previously generated caution. Whatever the emerging capacity, it's like the pain the kid is experiencing has purpose. It is pushing the new stage of growth. Since then, I always consider the eventual value of struggle whenever my kids are having a series of difficult days. What may have been a fleeting afterthought for that mom helped me shift my lens from frustration to patience at the right moment.

> Partnering with people in your community often doesn't require a formal arrangement. Unexpected connections can be surprisingly powerful when you open yourself up to them. But even casual exchanges call for some vulnerability on your part to best tap into their potential benefits. You don't always have to appear competent.

That can be uncomfortable, especially when you've imagined your struggle is unique or convinced yourself that you should already have the answers. If you catch yourself falling into that common trap, please remember: Nobody is a stranger to struggle. There's never any shame in voicing concerns or asking for help...and you just might be helping the other person as well.

All of us have had the experience of hoping our vulnerabilities remain hidden. Consider the last time you lost your temper after your kids pushed you to your last nerve. None of us are proud of those moments.

Sharing struggle is a choice to be vulnerable. As perfect as our social media portrayals of our families may be, the reality is that everyone stumbles. Everyone faces situations in which they don't know what to do. Reaching out for help is a silent acknowledgment of this truth.

THE IMPORTANCE OF PERSPECTIVE

Feeling vulnerable is normal when trying to make a change. Nobody enjoys being called out for exacerbating a problem, even if they are unaware they are doing so or acting with the best intentions (especially then!). And it's uncomfortable, at best, to think about shaking up well-established patterns and routines, even when they're not ideal.

It's this kind of tough stuff that usually deserves the most attention, but by virtue of its "toughness," it's also always the most distressing to discuss. It takes a certain amount of courage to address a sensitive issue. If you are feeling short of courage, rest assured the challenge will build it in you.

Like any other challenge you feel reluctant to tackle, you might have to force yourself to lean into thorny topics. An awareness of the sensitive nature of the subject matter and an ounce of preparation will help you on your way. Offer grace for one another throughout the process. Be patient and listen.

> *Try not to discount anyone's thoughts or ideas, and pace your responses until everything has been unpacked and laid out in front of you.*

When I'm faced with a prickly parenting or family challenge, it helps to remember that nobody is expected to see with perfect objectivity while they're immersed in a situation. I need everyone's perspective to get a clear picture, even when I'm resistant to ask for it. The more significant the challenge, the more this is true.

Being in the eye of the storm will always prevent my ability to grasp the true scope of it. What I'm experiencing feels all-encompassing, but it's only a portion. While I'm trying to get my husband to notice the flooding on the ground, he's wondering why I'm not seeing the car flying through the air. The flooding is important, but so is the car.

If you've ever navigated the ordinarily familiar hallways of your own home in the dark, you know what it's like to be immersed in a parenting situation full of unknowns. Even in the wee hours of the night, there is a small amount of light. You put your hands out to feel for walls and corners while extending your feet cautiously at the first and last step of the stairway.

Inevitably, however, you step on the Lego brick barefoot and let out a yelp that communicates both sharp pain and pent-up frustration with the child who didn't clean up their toys. There is always a blend of visible, marginally visible, and invisible obstacles. Fortunately, there is also always a blend of visible, marginally visible, and invisible enablers.

Of course, parenting and family challenges are not hurricanes or dark houses with Lego landmines. We have the benefit of time to survey the scene and build our awareness of the situation. The problem is that we often don't.

The common mode of operation in today's world is to feel rushed, harried, and overwhelmed by life, and then to vaguely wonder why we're not enjoying this parenting thing as much as we'd hoped we would. Let this book function as a guide to help you get back to a place where you can slow down, regroup, and have real conversations about the things that are begging for attention. Once you've honestly taken in all of the influencing factors of a challenge, you'll be in a much better position to set the stage for success.

ALL IN GOOD TIME

"There are years that ask questions and years that answer."
Zora Neale Hurston, *Their Eyes Were Watching God*

A year is a long time to wait, but certain understandings need time. We "get" things in our 30s differently than in our 20s. Some revelations and epiphanies take four or five decades to simmer. In fact, experts say true altruism doesn't unfold developmentally until our 60s.

It's clear that many elements of our journey can't be rushed. On the other hand, it feels more true than ever that some things can be addressed with quick action—solutions might even be just a click or a question to Siri or Alexa away. So, do we count on the promise of maturation or actively ignite our resources?

As Zora Neale Hurston reminds us, there is a season for everything. There's no getting around that. Still, what if we were able to translate years to weeks? What if we paid deliberate attention to the countless daily opportunities for growth and learning that the environment gifts us around the clock?

This book is designed to highlight the best places to aim your focus and the people you should partner with. Problem-solving, no matter the timeline, is at its best a collaboration—a collaboration with your child, your spouse, your kid's teachers and caregivers, and the host of professionals who can't wait to join your team.

"In a minute there can be an hour. In a second there can be a day."
Shawn Phillips, *"No Question"*

Find your moment. As a child, I used to imagine the ability to apply the brakes to good times to make them last and push the accelerator past difficult patches. I've since learned to do the opposite.

Slow down and understand the struggles and what lessons they are trying to teach us. Look pain straight in the eye and figure out its message. Then, allow the good times to feed eternity rather than attempting to stop the world or stamp the goodness into permanence.

Each day provides an opportunity to understand your child's behavior as a roadmap for navigating the particular challenge of the moment. Staying present in that moment is the key. It's way too easy to allow the situation to trigger past doubts or future anxieties. Instead, let the moment be your teacher.

> *Let's simplify. No matter what is happening in the environment, it's always either establishing your child's foundation, strengthening their ability to connect, enabling growth, or building resilience.*

When you stop to find your moment, you provide yourself the magic of turning a minute into an hour or a second into a day. You're letting yourself see the purpose of your circumstances, along with clues on how best to respond to your ever-changing environment. It's almost like you're giving yourself a chance to call time-out and calculate your strategy.

Now, let's go back to the F.E.A.T and bring it all together.

ESTABLISHING THE FOUNDATION, STRENGTHENING CONNECTION, ENABLING GROWTH, AND BUILDING RESILIENCE

This book is the companion piece to the assessment tool that I published with Steve Ritter in 2020. Since then, Steve and I have met with countless families in both mini-consults and extended co-led sessions that blend my occupational therapy and his social work skills. Despite the diverse array of clients we have served together, common themes abound.

CHAPTER 10: BRINGING IT ALL TOGETHER

These 10 themes can be applied to any family situation:

1. Regardless of the symptom triggering the engagement of our services, there is always an environmental component. It is never just the child having a problem. The struggle lives in the context of a larger story.

2. There is always a lens on your circumstances you haven't considered. Perspectives obvious to others, despite being under your nose, are only accessible when you widen the lens.

3. Most struggles become clear when you ask the question, "What would need to be true to make my child's behavior make sense?" The question forces you to look at the bigger picture.

4. Small changes make big differences. Difficult periods rarely need a complete overhaul. Usually, a small but strategic tweak sets things on a better course.

5. Adaptability and flexibility are key. Continuous changes are a given. Preparing for the ripple effect of change lets you benefit from the movement, rather than getting knocked off balance by it.

6. Children (and their parents!) always have a remarkable ability to rise to the challenge, no matter the struggle. Given the right blend of time, space, and support, progress inevitably follows. This is the meaning of resilience.

7. If nothing changes, nothing changes. The comfort of pouring cement around old patterns is in constant conflict with the courage to try something different. Experimentation usually leads to discovery even if the new idea doesn't work.

8. It's good to change your lens often. Zoom in and out. Study the particulars of your situation and then step back and put it in perspective. Some circumstances call for a telephoto lens while others need a wide-angle.

9. Your family's well-being is the heart of everything. It's the reason for the tough conversations and the late-night worry. When momentum stalls, it helps to bring this simple truth back into the spotlight.

10. Your instincts are trustworthy. It's easy to get muddled up in conflicting messages and feelings of uncertainty. Underneath all of that, your gut is already telling you exactly where to focus your energy.

These 10 common themes should point you in the right direction. Widening the lens is a way to see what might happen next if you reconsider your parenting strategy. Granted, no one has a crystal ball, least of all caregivers trying to predict a child's future.

But I can tell you one thing for certain: the fact that you're taking this time to consider the impact of the bigger picture on your child's experience is a clear indication you're already doing a good job of setting them up for success.

Understanding the state of your foundation, connection, growth, and resilience gives you a major advantage. However, understanding is only half the job. Taking the next steps to put your knowledge into action will do wonders for your child's ability to flourish and for your family's well-being.

You have the power to move mountains by shaping the environment to boost your child's learning, behavior, and development—one observation, one realization, one conversation, one decision, one change at a time.

Afterword

By identifying key influences on development and noting subtle changes in real time, families can strengthen each cycle of their child's development. The environment shapes learning and adaptation from the minute infants become aware of their surroundings. Tweaks can be made as development unfolds, but much is left up to chance when it's done without intention.

Everyone's behavior results from interactions between internal states and changing physical, emotional, and social environments.

This starts simply in the womb, when the developing fetus is shaped by prenatal conditions. Once the baby is born, the environment immediately takes on infinite new facets. Sights, sounds, smells, tastes, and touches begin teaching.

With the first breath, the child's experience of the environment begins influencing the way they behave, think, connect, grow, and process the world.

All people experience lifelong change, yet transitions during childhood tend to be more pronounced as internal development is still maturing. Even when all seems calm to an onlooker, the child's brain is in a busy state of learning and adjustment. Growth is a result of these continuous internal responses to external factors.

A healthy environment boosts growth and development. But even in the best conditions, kids' environments are always shifting. These changes are natural fuel for growth in every person's life. Unless environmental influences are identified and folded in, the full potential of any learning experience is lessened.

When you widen the lens, you put yourself in the position to see the hidden forces that shape kids.

Every day gives parents a reason to zoom in and look at their kids from close proximity. When we do this, important factors in our kids' development move into our blind spots. It's a form of benign neglect. We don't know what we don't know.

Stepping back and seeing a broader perspective brings the answers out of hiding.

Health, expectations, family dynamics, caregiver needs, developmental stage, enablers & obstacles, support systems, and *disposition* all ebb and flow as cyclical environmental influences in your child's world. From minute to minute, hour to hour, day to day, month to month, and year to year, a wide-angle view keeps parents and caregivers alert to the subtle drivers of learning and growth.

Raising kids is a complex endeavor. This book attempts to simplify the challenge. When you go back and re-read the annotations in the margins, dog-eared pages, and bookmarks, remember why those messages resonate with you. Take this book personally. It is designed to apply specifically to the unique circumstances of each reader and their own environmental situation.

Moreover, it is crafted to provide different answers to different questions as your family situation evolves. Keep this book and the companion F.E.A.T. resource handy and open them whenever the path forward isn't clear. The reference section of your home library is a good location for the "why" of the F.E.A.T. resource and the "how" of *Widen the Lens*.

When you are in the dark, this book will be the flashlight.

The accepted motto of parenting is that it's the hardest and most rewarding job anyone will ever have. When times get tough, we so often slump our shoulders, nod our heads, and remind ourselves it's just part of the deal. My greatest hope is that you'll shift your idea slightly about that first part, the part that implies resignation to an uphill struggle fraught with hardship. It needn't be a struggle you sit with.

Each of us has felt lost at times. When we're in a part of the woods we've never been before, it's so difficult to find a way out. Please use the ideas you've found here to keep from spinning in circles when the parenting terrain is wild and overgrown and nothing feels familiar.

There's always a path forward when you widen the lens enough to understand the landscape.

Acknowledgments

The seeds for this book were planted more than 20 years ago, when life circumstances intersected with my love for environmental science and psychology. These seeds germinated and flourished in an ecosystem of supportive mentorships and partnerships that were instrumental in guiding and course-correcting me. But most of all, they were essential in nudging me forward when my own confidence was not strong enough to keep me moving by myself.

It, therefore, comes as no surprise to the readers of this book that I apply the principles of environmental assessment and action to my life on a daily basis. I can only hope to support others the way I have been supported throughout this journey. As such, I would like to thank the following family, friends, neighbors, and colleagues for your impact on my wellness and clarity. Each of them, whether they realize it or not, has been a co-author of this book.

Jamie, your steadfast devotion is second to none. You never once complained about all of the times I woke you by creeping out of bed before dawn to write at an ungodly hour, or all of the times I was half-awake during the evening as a result. Thank you for being my eternal partner in all the good, bad, and ugly that comes from parenting. I promise to work on returning to a normal sleep schedule so we can hang out after sunset again.

Ben, Sam, and Theo, thanks to you, the concepts in these pages are more than just theory. Nothing has made me a better therapist (or person) than the experience of being your mom. You continue to teach me, humble me, and delight me in more ways than I could describe in even 10 zillion pages.

Steve Ritter, without you there would be no book at all, and I might have ended up a despondent librarian. For your infinite nudges, tireless collaboration, and generous spirit, I'm forever indebted.

To all the other people who read early versions or offered thoughtful *discussion or shaped my thinking in ways they may not even realize, I thank you: Kathy Barry, Dick Brundage, Evan Brundage, Gwyneth Brundage, Joanne Brundage, Zach Brundage, Cindy Choi, Doreen Comings, Louie Chua, Tina Czerwinski, Katie Delaney, Benny Delgado, Chrissy Delgado, Mary Lou Eisenhauer, Kerry Fallon, Nancy Funk, Amy Galarza, John Galarza, Linda Galarza, Robert Galarza, Sarah Galarza, William Galarza, Christin Henkel, Dawn Hoelzer, Darcy Josephson, Meghan Kamperschroer, Markus Kirschner, Weykyoi Victor Kore, Sue Kuchta, Robin Lacey, Kerri Matusek, Mike Matusek, Katie McDougall-Powers, Scott Mies, Cara Milianti, Rachel Morris, the entire Myrtle Avenue Posse, Laxmi Narayan, Beth Neal, Nancy Nega, Miriam Newett, Tom Newett, Kelly Novak, Bryan O'Donnell, Kim O'Hare, Anne Papineau, Rick Prangen, Laura Rees, Nancy Ritter, Laura Rodey, Angie Soto, Monica Soto, Ann Spirakis, Rachel Surprenant, Dana Steinecker, Lora Valentin, Rosalee Washington, Alissa Zahorak, Michele Zelinski, and Liz Zomchek.*

About the Author

KERRY GALARZA, MS OTR/L is a pediatric occupational therapist and the Clinical Director of the Midwest Institute & Center for Workplace Innovation. She provides specialized assessment and intervention with children of all ages and their families. Kerry engages clients with naturally occurring, meaningful home-based methods to empower autonomy and maximize functioning. While providing focused experience in sensory processing disorder and the autism spectrum, Kerry partners with the network of professionals collaborating in the targeted care of each child's circumstances. Kerry also provides family-centered occupational therapy services addressing a range of developmental delays in collaboration with the Illinois Early Intervention Program.

Earning her bachelor's degree in Environmental Sciences and a Master's degree in Occupational Therapy from the University of Illinois, along with extensive training and an Associate's degree in Psychology from the Chicago School of Professional Psychology, Kerry specializes in helping her clients navigate the impact of the environment on their ability to thrive holistically.

Made in the USA
Columbia, SC
25 August 2021